Getting

into

POTS

A Basic Pottery Manual

GEORGE & NANCY WETTLAUFER

Prentice-Hall, Inc.
Englewood Cliffs, New Jersey

Library of Congress Cataloging in Publication Data

Wettlaufer, George.
   Getting into pots: a beginning pottery manual.

   Bibliography: p.
   Includes index.
   1. Pottery craft.   I. Wettlaufer, Nancy, joint
author.   II. Title.
TT920.W45   738.1   76–20643
ISBN 0–13–354712–4
ISBN 0–13–354704–3 pbk.

Large Cover Photo: (Fig. 7–18 in interior)
Porcelain teapot with cane bail handle: Wood-fired.
Ruth McKinley, Canada, 1973. (*Courtesy of the artist*)
(*Photograph by Donald Lloyd McKinley*)

10   9   8   7   6   5   4   3

Printed in the United States of America

PRENTICE-HALL INTERNATIONAL, INC., *London*
PRENTICE-HALL OF AUSTRALIA PTY. LIMITED, *Sydney*
PRENTICE-HALL OF CANADA, LTD., *Toronto*
PRENTICE-HALL OF INDIA PRIVATE LIMITED, *New Delhi*
PRENTICE-HALL OF JAPAN, INC., *Tokyo*
PRENTICE-HALL OF SOUTHEAST ASIA PTE. LTD., *Singapore*
WHITEHALL BOOKS LIMITED, *Wellington, New Zealand*

Contents

Preface

This is more than a down-to-earth pottery book for beginners: We have tried to show what happens when people "meet" pots. It is a how-to-work-with-clay book and also a how-to-make-decisions book—consumer decisions about buying equipment and materials that are appropriate to your goals and your stage of development. And some "hows," "whys," and "do's and don'ts" are included.

Although we are full-time production potters ourselves, this book is intended both for beginners getting into pots as a hobby and for art teachers teaching pottery in the schools. It is a basic book that can be used effectively by total beginners with no prior instruction; it is also a "progressive" method, starting from the beginning and working through stages to a mastery of the basic skills. Our methods have been tested repeatedly on our own students, who, after eight weeks of lessons (two hours a week), understand the basics of throwing on the wheel and have some remarkably good pots to show for their efforts (see Figs. I-1 and I-2).

In several respects, this general pottery book is somewhat different from others on the market. *It gives as much emphasis to the people working with clay as to the finished pots.* In fact, the whole book is written almost as if the reader were sitting in the studio talking over his ideas or problems with us and listening to our reactions.

In line with this people-oriented philosophy, we have stayed away from museum collections of pots for our photos. Pots are to be used and enjoyed. All the pots in this book exist in people's homes—our own, their creator's, or friends' of their creators. There are pots being used every day in people's homes that equal or excel in beauty those behind glass or in museum storerooms. And pots are a kind of presence that remind you of the person who made them—like having friends in your home with you. Museum pots tend to lack this additional dimension. We have also included candid photos of our students, enjoying themselves with clay up to their elbows, and of our children, who were 5½ and 7 when this manuscript was written—all enjoyed working on the wheel and achieving some measure of success.

Our basic backgrounds and experiences are less "traditional" than those of the authors of most pottery books—neither of us was trained in an art school. George's training as a ceramic engineer turned out to be extremely helpful technically but is not a normal entry into the pottery world. Nancy was a French and German teacher originally—a seemingly far cry from the eventual outcome but also a useful orientation. Teaching any skill—language or pottery—requires an ability to break it down into small component parts and then put it back into a whole again. As far removed as it sounds, teaching the skills of wheel-throwing is not that different from teaching the skills of language.

In a way, *our background may be more sympathetic to our readers,* especially those who have had little or no formal schooling in art or pottery and are figuring clay out for themselves. In the long run, it was probably just as well that we didn't know what we were supposed to be doing—as a result, we developed a style that was our own with little temptation to imitate someone else. George developed our clay body and glazes for electric kiln firing (see Section II) when it was still a hobby and again later for the gas kiln. And since we had never been taught to fire a gas kiln the right way, he also developed a new method of measuring and controlling reduction. This is proving itself an extremely useful tool for others learning to fire gas kilns on their own and is attracting a lot of interest on the part of ceramics teachers.

We are also more oriented to the marketplace than the traditional art teacher giving ceramics instruction. Some of the hurdles of getting into pots for most readers may involve the consumer-type decisions facing them. What kind of wheel should I get? Do I need a kiln, or will somebody fire my pots for me? If I need a kiln, what kind? How much will this equipment cost? What about materials; where do I get them? Should I plan to buy or mix my own clay, glazes, etc.? Since we too, not long ago, had to go through this same evaluation, and since our beginning students are now asking the same questions, we have tried to define your problems and give you a lot of basic consumer information and advice —including shopping lists for materials and equipment and lists of suppliers.

A progressive approach. *Section I, Getting into Clay,* is divided into ten chapters, the first eight of which are labeled "lessons," because they are actual class presentations. They can each be accomplished in one 2-hour class session and are, in essence, the lesson plans we have very carefully developed and tested with our own students. The following chapters contain useful information, presented in a progressive order, that the reader, who has already mastered (or soon will) the basic skills, can digest at will.

In Section I, we provide very detailed instruction on mastering the techniques of wheel-throwing—almost a programmed learning approach and self-teachable, although having an instructor makes it much easier. We have emphasized wheel-throwing over handbuilding for several reasons:

1. Because it is what we do ourselves and how we make our living, so it's what we know best.

2. Wheel-throwing seems to be the fascination that attracts many people to pottery as a hobby—almost as if mastering the wheel were a new sport, like tennis or skiing.

3. The basics of handbuilding can, with an initial understanding of the method, be self-taught and experimented with more successfully than can wheel-throwing—there is no new physical coordination involved. This is not to suggest that it is any less demanding to make a good pot by means of handbuilding than by throwing; in some respects it is more difficult, due to the freedom involved and the lack of mechanical limitations that the wheel automatically imposes. Most people who are interested can get into handbuilding more easily on their own—with a few basic concepts and some inspiration from photos. A good deal of specific instruction is needed, followed by diligent practice, to break into throwing.

The basics for both wheel-throwing and handbuilding methods are presented in Section I. The teacher or individual working with the book must adapt his concentration on one or the other to suit his own purposes.

We encourage beginners especially to plan to fire in an electric kiln (see *Section II, Getting into Firing*)—you may have to anyway if you're taking classes in school— at least until you have learned what firing and glazing are all about. And we have provided you with some easy (surprisingly so) glaze recipes that require only four or five common materials and give surprisingly good results. Friends and art teachers all over have been using them and vouch for their ease of mixing as well as their consistent results. They're also much cheaper and much better than the commercially mixed glazes. The main thing, though, is that they work. In fact, everything in the book works—we know from experience that it does. We have refrained from telling you how things ought to be and have stuck to how things are in the real world. Being creative with clay depends to a large measure on understanding your materials, knowing what is available, and knowing how to work within the limitations imposed by the clay itself and/or by the equipment you must work with.

Section III, Getting in a Little Further, is a "stretch" section. You may not be ready for it at first. However, if you are not a beginner, you may be especially interested in our method of measuring and controlling reduction, our ideas about making a living and selling pottery (excerpted and condensed from our first book), or our design for a homemade slab roller that is inexpensive and really works. There is also material on pouring plaster, photographing pottery, teaching ceramics in school art classes, and odds and ends of useful information that are, in most cases, too advanced for the very beginner but useful to the potter with a little more experience or the teaching potter. Perhaps it will help to give the beginner an idea of where he may eventually be headed.

There is no way to cover everything in detail when you are writing a general book. For this reason, we have included a bibliography, a list of suppliers, additional glaze recipes, a glossary of materials, and a glossary of terms. If you are interested in an aspect of pottery that we have not covered in detail, we hope we have given you enough information to pursue it elsewhere. And we hope that what we've written is helpful to the many people who are fascinated by pottery and interested in "getting into pots" on their own.

We would like to make a strange kind of offer as well. If you are having a problem —with your glazes, your firing, your clay body, whatever—can't seem to get to the bottom of it on your own, and aren't quite sure where to turn, write to us. (Send a stamped self-addressed envelope.) George is a good pot doctor and likes being a diagnostician. He really enjoys solving technical problems, especially when they are someone else's, and we enjoy hearing from people. We certainly don't know everything, but we'll try to help if we can.

ACKNOWLEDGMENTS

Special thanks are due:

—first and foremost to our photographer, Rob Howard
—to D. Dana Robinson for the line drawings
—to our friend, Jean Delius, who allowed us to photograph her outstanding pottery collection
—to those potters who submitted photos or let us photograph their work
—to Marie Hewett of the Carborundum Museum of Ceramics
—to our pottery students, who were willing students, and
—to our children, who put up with us while we were involved in this project.

We think we should also thank Hank Kennedy of Prentice-Hall, who started all this when he came to borrow our trailer hitch one day and left with his eternal question, "Why don't you write a book?" Much to everyone's surprise, this turned out to be more than rhetorical.

GEORGE AND NANCY WETTLAUFER
12 E. Lake Street
Skaneateles, New York 13152

Getting into Clay

SECTION

I

Introduction

OUR LESSONS

When we first began making pots for a living (having done it for a while as a hobby), we were pretty flexible about what we would do to make ends meet. One summer, a friend offered to pay us for instruction on the wheel. We agreed—why not? Gradually that summer, five or six more people began coming for private lessons. Things went pretty smoothly until late fall, when it was time to get ready for Christmas sales. As Christmas approached, we found ourselves frantically trying to get our own pots made and being interrupted by the private lessons. We were still doing all of our work in our house at that time, since the barn-studio wasn't heated yet, glazing up kilns-full of pots in the kitchen on card tables and trying to finish up before it was time to get supper. On top of all this, we were constantly running up and down stairs to check on students working in our cellar "studio." Finally it dawned on us that there had to be a better way—giving private lessons at Christmas time was certainly a mistake.

So, we called off the private instruction and told everybody to wait until spring when we'd have a new set-up. After Christmas, we had time to think it over and we decided to take a chance and invest in five inexpensive (under $200) electric wheels. We insulated the barn and added a good heater. And set up our present eight-week course system of small class instruction (7 students). Rather than fit private students into our own pace of production, we used the lessons as a change of pace entirely. The first year we gambled that we could fill at least five classes of six students (we had six wheels and wanted to make sure each student had his own wheel). To our surprise and relief, we had about forty-five people sign up, including enough for two classes for children—starting at age 9.

We've found this system has worked very well, and the students are generally pleased with what they learn and accomplish in eight weeks. Occasionally students show up expecting to make a complete dinner set and all the planters they'll need for gifts for the next year. They're disappointed when we tell them they'll only be able to fire their five best pieces. But by the end of the course, when they've managed a crude mug with an even cruder handle, perhaps a pitcher, a covered jar and a small planter, they realize that five pots are a *lot*. (See Figs. I-1 and I-2.)

Some of our students have had a little experience; some are back taking lessons for a second time; most are pure beginners. Usually we keep them all in the same class, going over the basics step-by-step. The repeaters absorb much more the second time around, and the beginners get a chance to see where they might be headed.

We have discovered that most of our students aren't very interested in learning about glazing and firing. They want to spend their time working at the wheel—making things—and would just as soon leave the rest to us. So we wait until later to teach it.

We also teach the basics of handbuilding and encourage students to take clay home to try a slab or coil pot on their own—since it requires no special equipment like a wheel. Later on, we get out the Raku clay and have them pinch some pots at home so we can have a Raku party some Saturday. This turns out to be a lot of fun, and a lot of learning takes place, too.

OUR STUDENTS

Understandably, beginning students arrive for pottery lessons with a number of misconceptions about the materials, techniques, and equipment involved, such as:

1. Pottery lessons will be similar to hobby ceramics classes.

Both can be referred to as "ceramics," creating some confusion.

2. Doing it yourself will save money.

Fig. I-1 Covered jars (stopper style lids).

Fig. I-2 First teapots.

Most of our students end up making three or four little pots after paying us $50.00 (presently) for eight lessons—hardly a bargain as far as purchasing pottery goes. If you intend to buy a wheel and kiln, or build your own equipment, you can expect to spend upwards of $1000 to set up a studio. This doesn't include the materials and fuel you will be paying for regularly, at an ever-increasing cost. *Generalization #1:* If you like pottery and want to *have* pots, *buy them from potters.* You'll get more variety and, at first anyway, better quality at much less cost.

3. You are going to sit right down at the wheel and make all the planters, teapots, or dinner plates you need.

One girl who ran a plant store even thought she could make the planters to go with the plants they were selling—after one eight-week session. *Generalization #2:* You are learning a skill—like learning to play the piano—which takes constant practice. The end product of pottery lessons (at least ours) is a degree of mastery over the techniques involved in working with clay and some knowledge about its properties and behavior.

What happens at the end of eight weeks is that we've taught a little bit of pottery and a lot of pottery appreciation. Often our students end up becoming some of our best customers. And whether they buy pots from us or another potter, their lessons have given them an awareness of the complexities involved in making a pot and make them better consumers of the pottery sold at craft fairs or in shops.

What do our students do after they take our classes? Some do go on, get their own wheels, and find a place to fire their work. We have both kick wheels and electric wheels in our studio, so they can see what each is like before they invest in their own equipment. We also have a small electric kiln and a larger gas kiln, so they can see the different types of kilns. Being able to see both the kinds of equipment and the processes involved gives them a good idea of whether they want to set up their own studios or not. Many find they would just as soon come back once a year and take lessons.

Occasionally people ask us if we rent out studio space—we don't because we need all our space and can't afford interruptions when we're working. But many places are beginning to rent space both for throwing and for firing. For the occasional potter, this may be a better solution than investing in expensive equipment that won't be used frequently.

Here's our studio set-up. We've found it works very well, and it can be adapted for use in a school setting or a small workshop:

Six small electric wheels (Spinning Tigers) on cinder blocks with cinder blocks for seats

One kick wheel (Randall)

A pug mill for reclaiming clay

A garbage can full of student clay (we go through close to 1,000 pounds)

One wareboard per class and a roll of plastic that we can tear off to cover the pots on each wareboard to keep them moist for a week (a "damp box" of sorts)

A bucket of water for throwing—and later for washing up (we don't have running water in the barn)

A bucket for sloppy clay water when finished throwing

Another garbage can for dry pots that are being discarded and will be reclaimed

A bucket for soggy mushed pots—to go back through the pug mill with the addition of some more ball clay to stiffen it back up

Tools and sponges for everybody

(Some day we'll install showers for cleaning up afterwards)

Here's an outline of the eight-week course we give in our studio. It can easily

be adapted to a one-semester beginning course in a high school or adult education class. It is really a method—not just a bunch of projects—based on positive help at all stages and the philosophy that if people understand clearly what they are trying to do, they will be able to do it. If students learn first what a centered ball of clay feels like, and if you (the teacher) help them center it at first so they get used to working on a centered piece of clay, gradually and almost automatically they discover they are centering their own clay without a lot of frustration.

This is the order in which we present the basics of throwing (two-hour classes).

1. First Week—Getting Started
    a. Inspection of our pottery collection and viewing of our slides of pots and how to make them
    b. Introduction to other methods— slab, coil, pinch
    c. Getting the feel of clay on the wheel
2. Second Week—The Basic Cylinder
    a. Wedging
    b. Working through the steps of making a pot (see Figs. I-3 and I-4)

Fig. I-4 Our students learning to pull a basic cylinder.

Fig. I-3 Centering.

   c. Save a pot for trimming next week

3. Third Week—Leather-Hard Pots
   a. Trimming
   b. Decorating with texture and engobes (on last week's pot)
   c. Throw a taller mug-shaped-cylinder to keep for handles next week

4. Fourth Week—Pulling and Attaching Handles
   a. Learn to pull handles
   b. Trim pot made last week
   c. Make a new pot for another handle next week—a mug or a pitcher
   d. Attach the handle made at the beginning of class to the mug made last week

5. Fifth Week—Mostly Review; Introduction to Lids
   a. Trouble-shooting review—work a pot through in unison again and discuss problem areas
   b. Shape control—for making a pitcher with curved sides
   c. Throw a pot that a cork will fit into as a "lid"

6. Sixth Week—Covered Jars
   a. Demonstration of three different types of jars and their lids
   b. Students throw a jar and lid
   c. Trim pots made the previous week if any and attach handles

7. Seventh Week—Teapots
   a. Anchoring lids or irregular shapes for trimming
   b. Constructing a teapot

8. Eighth Week—Glazing
   a. Prepare bisque-fired pots by sanding, signing with satin, and waxing areas not to be glazed
   b. Applying glaze

(We fire the students' pots and they return in two weeks to pick them up.)

Somewhere along the way—about the fourth week—we give students some Raku clay, show them how to pinch good solid forms and have them do some pinch pots at home, which they bring back for bisque-firing prior to the Saturday Raku party.

LESSON **1**

Getting Started

As our students arrive for the first time, we encourage them to look around our house at all the pots—some made by us, some by other potters; some made on the wheel, some handbuilt. We tell them to pick up the pots, inspect them, feel them, and try to figure out how they were made.

Then, after some introductions and nitty-gritty-type bookkeeping, we show them slides—us making a pot from start to finish, last year's classes working and some of their finished work, and the Raku party with everybody having fun. That way everybody has a little better idea of what is going to be involved in the coming weeks—*before* we go out to the studio. This type of introduction can easily be adapted to a school situation.

WAYS TO MAKE POTS

Although our students are anxious to get to the wheels, we think it's important for them to know different methods of constructing pots. We show them samples of pots made by coiling, slab-building, pinching, *and* throwing. That way they can see how each different construction method works and how each produces a different kind of pot (Fig. 1-1).

Introduction to Handbuilding. Before we go to the wheel, we talk about the three nonwheel methods of constructing pots—these are called *handbuilding*.

Coiling. Coiling is probably the oldest and most universal method potters have

Fig. 1-1 Cylinders made with four different techniques: slab, coil, pinch, and wheel.

Fig. 1-2 Coiled bowl; Southwest Indian pottery. *(Courtesy Sue and Herb Carson)*

used to make functional ware—bowls, storage jars, and other large pieces—without a wheel. Most American Indian pots (Fig. 1-2) were made by coiling, then smoothed out and decorated.

To coil a pot, start by breaking off a piece of clay. Roll it between your hands to start the coil; then roll it flat on a table top with your fingers—between your first and second joints—to the desired length and thickness (Fig. 1-3). Roll out a batch of coils before you begin constructing—it's easier to get into a rhythm that way.

Make the base of your pot by flattening a ball of clay with your hands (or by rolling out a slab and cutting it, or by pinching an open bowl shape). It does not necessarily have to be round—oval coil pots are especially interesting and look less wheel-like (Fig. 1-4).

Fig. 1-3 Rolling a coil.

Fig. 1-4 Applying slip after scoring base of coil pot.

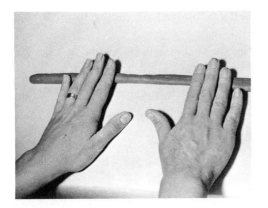

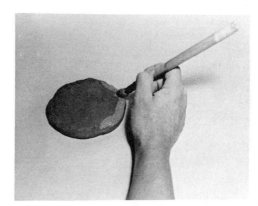

Fig. 1-5 Attaching coil to base.

Fig. 1-6 Adding coils.

Fig. 1-7 Vertical rim decoration with wood tool.

Then add the coils. It's best to cross-hatch or score each layer of coils with a hacksaw blade or other pointed tool, add slip clay, and weld each layer into the preceding one with your fingers or a tool.

Fig. 1-8 Coil teapot; Skip Lyman. Coil construction, white clay decorated and stained to emphasize construction. (*Courtesy Jean Delius*)

Do this on the inside if you want the coiled effect to remain as decoration on the outside—showing how the pot was constructed. Or you can smooth all the coils in and scrape the pot with a metal rib when it's leather hard, leaving a natural shape but no sign of coils (Figs. 1-5, 1-6, and 1-7).

Fairly complex forms such as a teapot can be made by this method (Fig. 1-8).

Children especially like rolling coils for a single group pot. Each student, with help, can come and attach his two or three coils to the pot (Fig. 1-9). The thicknesses will vary, but they can be worked in. Children may enjoy putting the coils on in funny patterns, instead of coiling them around

Fig. 1-9 First graders constructing a class coil pot.

horizontally. Many are also very good at modeling little animals to add to the pot afterwards.

Slab Construction. Joining slabs of clay is another handbuilding technique. It's very versatile and can be used to make anything from square boxes to tall, graceful planters.

Rolling out a slab of clay to work with is like rolling out a pie crust. You can use your kitchen rolling pin—the ball bearing kind works easiest (Fig. 1-10).

Put a piece of cloth (like burlap) on a table to prevent sticking. To get an even thickness, put two rulers or any two boards of even thickness on either side of the clay. Then roll out the clay.

Look around your kitchen for bowls, plates, bottles, etc., which you can use to drape the clay over or around as a basic mold or support. Later, you may want to make your own drape molds from plaster.

Look in your utensil drawer for things to press into the clay to make interesting textures. Potato mashers, forks, garlic squeezers, etc., will all do very well.

Or try going for a walk to collect natural objects—nuts, leaves, seeds, pine cones, shells, etc. (Figs. 1-11, 1-12, and 1-13). Look around you—and play.

Fig. 1-10 Rolling a slab.

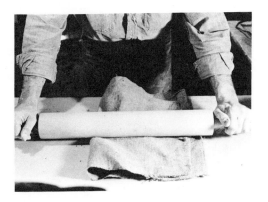

Fig. 1-11 Inge and Kurt texturing their slab.

Fig. 1-12 Sample texture tiles, class assignment, Pensacola Junior College, Florida.

Fig. 1-13 Found objects impressed into a soft slab of clay.

Fig. 1-14 Sandwiching two slabs of clay—the top curved slab has been textured by rolling grass into it and then allowing it to set up over a form before being joined to the base.

Fig. 1-15 Rolling a slab over a form to construct a cylinder.

Fig. 1-16 Attaching bottom.

Fig. 1-17 Joining rectangular slabs.

Fig. 1-18 Constructing a "box" shape with leather-hard rectangles.

How you think of the rolled out slab of clay will determine how to work with it (Fig. 1-14). If you work with a slab when it's still fairly soft, think of it as fabric and you'll get soft, curved shapes (Figs. 1-15 and 1-16). If you let it dry some—to almost leather hard—think of it as a solid sheet of wood. Cut the slabs into rectangles and construct boxes or square vases or lamp bases from them (Figs. 1-17, 1-18, and 1-19). Thrown knobs or cylinders can often be added to slab pots for an interesting effect.

Remember to score and slip all edges when you attach anything. This will make the joint strong.

If you begin doing lots of slab pieces, you may be interested in our design for a home-made (and inexpensive) slab roller. It will give you large, even slabs with less effort. See p. 164 for how to build it.

Figures 1-20 through 1-25 are photos of slab work.

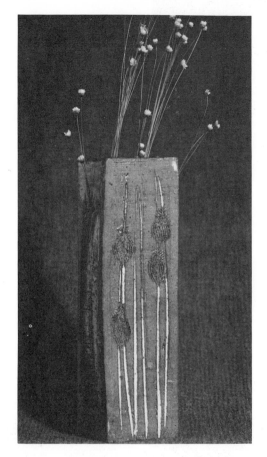

Fig. 1-19 The finished "box."

Fig. 1-20 Slab form; Don Reitz. Salt glazed. (*Courtesy Jean Delius*)

Fig. 1-21 Broadly textured slab planter; Ken Madakura, Canada (*Courtesy Ron McNie*)

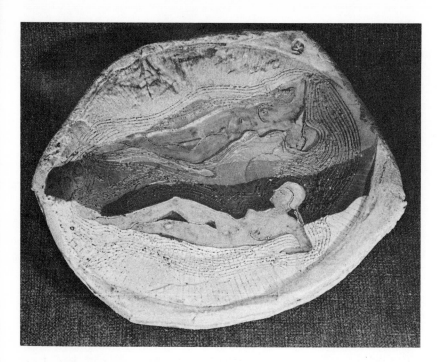

Fig. 1-22 Platter; Paul Soldner. Large slab with nudes in relief. (*Courtesy Jean Delius*)

Fig. 1-23 Slab-built porcelain flower arranging vase; Ruth McKinley, Canada, 1973. Celedon glaze, sprigged decoration, cone 10-11 reduction, wood-fired. (*Courtesy of the artist*) (*Photo by D. L. McKinley*)

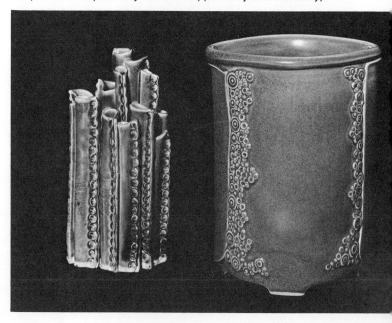

Fig. 1-24 Hollow form; Richard Zakin. Incised and stained, interior glazed only.

Fig. 1-25 Bottle; Bernard Leach. Slab construction with thrown neck. (*Courtesy Jean Delius*)

Pinching. Pinching is the third form of handbuilding. Although no wheel is used, it is similar to throwing in that you start with a wedged ball of clay and open it up by pressing your thumb into the center. After you open the ball of clay, gradually shape the pot by pressing your right thumb out against your cupped left hand, revolving the pot and thinning the walls. This is a very relaxing way of working with clay—one that makes you really feel as if you're "breathing life" into a lump of clay (Figs. 1-26, 1-27, and 1-28).

Small natural bowls are the easiest shapes to pinch. These work beautifully for raku firing and are consistent with the nature of raku.

Different-colored pieces of clay can also be flattened onto the outside of your

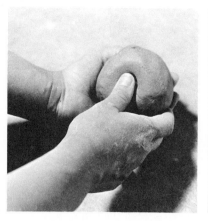

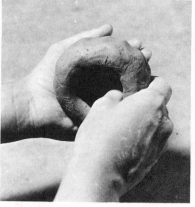

Fig. 1-26 Opening a pinch pot.

Fig. 1-27 Pinching out the hollow form.

Fig. 1-28 Thumb impressions as decoration on rim.

original ball of clay. In pinching the pot, you will marble the colored clay into the basic clay in soft natural patterns. Glazed with a clear glaze, these simple pinch pots with colored clays are very effective.

More complex forms can be made by joining several pinched sections together Two pinched pots joined at their rims will make a closed form that can be rolled or paddled into shape, then cut apart to make a covered jar. *Remember:* Score and apply slip to the edges whenever joining clay pieces.

Paulus Berensohn's book *Finding One's Way with Clay* is excellent for both the spirit and technique of pinching. If you're interested in making pinch pots, it is well worth reading.

Introduction to Throwing on the Wheel. Throwing on the wheel gives round, symmetrical shapes, as opposed to the freer, more natural shapes possible with handbuilding. If you've already done some handbuilding before you sit down at the wheel, you'll know what the clay feels like in your hands and between your fingers.

An important part of learning to throw on the wheel is getting correct "feelings" in your hands and body from the start. Beginning pottery students will encounter many new feelings as they go along. It is even a good idea to close your eyes and think about the messages your fingers and hands are sending to your brain: feelings like slippery-sticky, soft-hard, wobbly-centered. During the first lesson, I try to let the students feel their way through making a pot: learning where their body should be, how the clay should feel, what it's like to pull up a wall of a pot, etc. At this stage, I don't explain *what* I'm doing or *how* I'm doing it, but I simply have them feel each step involved after I complete it.

1. *Clay consistency:* I pass around three balls of clay that have been wedged-up and patted smooth—about snowball size or a little larger. One ball of clay is too soft for throwing; one is too stiff—almost brittle; the third is good for working on the wheel. That way, students can find out right away what plastic clay should feel like before they ever sit down at the wheel.

2. *Centeredness:* I plop a ball of clay on

18

the wheel head and get the wheel going at the right speed for centering. First, I have the students, one at a time, but still standing next to the wheel, put a hand on the clay and feel how much drag or friction there is before the clay has been wet—and how wobbly and unstable it feels. Then I quickly center the clay, having wet it first with a few drops of water from a sponge. I have the students feel the difference: Smooth, slippery, no drag, no wobbles. Now they know what wet, centered clay should feel like.

3. *Body position:* One by one, the students take my place sitting at the wheel. After wetting their hands and anchoring their elbows on their knees, they place their hands lightly around the revolving, centered ball of clay. We talk about being relaxed, steady, and keeping their hands stationary in front of them. Before they get up from the wheel, I put my hands over theirs and show them where to apply pressure when they go to center their own clay.

4. *Depth of floor of the pot:* After letting them feel the centered ball of clay, I open it with my thumbs to the proper depth, and then have them feel this— putting one finger on the hole and one on the bat outside—trying to judge the difference.

5. *Pulling up walls:* I slow down the wheel and have each student sit back down at the wheel in my spot. Then I put my hands over theirs and raise the wall, using their fingers.

6. *Thinness and evenness of walls:* After the students have felt the pulled-up wall with their fingers, we cut it down the center with a string so they can see if it looks as thin as it feels and to see if it has the same thickness top to bottom.

7. *The whole thing:* I take another ball of clay, center it, and work it through from start to finish in thirty seconds—one motion flowing into another, using no more than three pulls on the walls. This lets them see and feel how quickly and directly a pot can be made on the wheel and how rhythmic it is.

Once we've been through the steps, each student takes a ball of clay I've already wedged-up to his wheel. We learn how to use the equipment, and I tell them a few general rules to observe while working in our studio.

GENERAL RULES

1. Turn off the electric wheels when you're not using them and before you leave —at the switch. Keep the splash pans cleaned out as you're working so no clay gets in under the wheel head.

2. Keep track of your sponge! It's the same color as the clay and has a way of getting thrown into the slop bucket and being reclaimed right into the next batch of clay you'll be using. Once you try making a pot with a sponge in it, you'll understand.

3. Sign all pots—somewhere. Pots have a way of "changing" their size and appearance from one week to the next.

4. Don't handle anybody else's pots— greenware (dry clay) is very fragile.

5. Leave time for clean-up at the end of class—leave the studio as clean as you found it—or cleaner.

6. Cut your fingernails before class.

LESSON 2

Pulling the Basic Cylinder

WEDGING THE CLAY

Preparing the clay for throwing is called *wedging,* and it is very important. Spiral wedging is similar to kneading bread. Its purpose is to get all the air pockets out and to make the ball of clay one uniform consistency. (See Fig. 2-2.) It is usually done on a plaster wedging table, but it can be done on a counter covered with burlap to prevent sticking. Wedging isn't difficult once you learn how, but it is a skill which takes practice. Even an expert can't throw a pot with poorly wedged clay, so persist.

We have our students practice wedging their own clay from the start. But we always wedge up the first two or three balls of clay the students will be using while learning to throw to give them a fighting chance.

Have the chunk of clay to be wedged right in front of you. If you're wedging a large piece of clay, it helps to stand with one foot behind the other so you can get more strength from your shoulders and whole body pressing against the clay.

With the heels of both hands, press down onto the top of the clay; then, with your finger tips, reverse the motion, and pull the clay back toward you, at the same time twisting it slightly with your finger tips. The second time you press, it will be in a new place. Continue to press down, lift back and twist the clay in a rhythmic motion. Keep the clay in a snail-shaped ball within your hands—do not let it flatten out on the wedging table. (Most beginners press down too hard with the heels of their hands, smushing the clay all over the plaster table.) Press and rock gradually—eventually you will get to all portions of the ball of clay, and all possible air pockets will be expelled.

How Do I Know When I'm Done? Well, it doesn't usually take ten minutes, like kneading bread is supposed to, but there is no real way of telling a beginner when he's done—it has to "feel right." The best way to check is to take a piece of string and cut through the middle of the ball of clay—if there are no air pockets in this cross section, your clay is probably wedged enough. If you wedge up one large piece of clay and cut it into three or four smaller (one pound) balls—checking for air pockets with each cut—you'll have enough clay to last for an entire class without having to go back and wedge again. Pat these pieces into round snowballs without any creases; this is important later on, because creases in the ball of clay tend to turn into cracks in the bottom of your pot.

Wedging not only prepares your clay—it can prepare your head as well. Its rhythmic nature calms you down and gets you

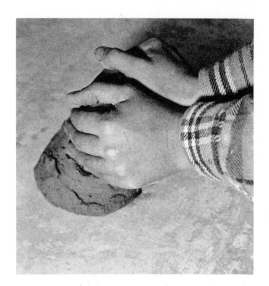

Fig. 2-2 Wedging.

thinking about what you will do with your clay on the wheel. When your pot is thrown "in your head," you've probably wedged your clay long enough and are ready to sit down at the wheel, forget the outside world you just left, and concentrate on throwing a pot.

Fig. 2-1 Cylinders from the authors' collection.

THROWING THE BASIC CYLINDER

Once the clay is prepared for throwing, I quickly demonstrate the procedure for throwing a simple pot. Then we all sit down at the wheels to work through each step together—with the intention of making a small pot, about as tall as it is wide, maybe 3″ x 3″, to carry through and trim in the leather-hard stage the following week. This is partly a review of material presented in Lesson 1. If you've forgotten, go back to p. 18 to refresh your memory.

Centering.

Step 1. With a jerk of your wrist throw your lump of clay down hard onto your bat (or metal wheel head), which has been *slightly* dampened with a sponge. Aim it at the center; if you miss by a lot, push and pat your lump of clay until it looks close to the center. Press down on it to make sure it's anchored and won't come off in your hands as soon as you start to squeeze it.

Step 2. Forget your hands for a moment, and activate the wheel with your foot. With the electric wheels, set the foot pedal at the right speed for centering (close to 180 r.p.m.'s); take your foot off the pedal and leave it alone while you're throwing.

Step 3. Wet your sponge and dribble water over your ball of clay until it's shiny —but don't drown it.

Step 4. With your feet flat on the floor —or well-anchored—rest your elbows on your knees so they feel very solid.

Step 5. Wet your hands (it's easier not to hold the sponge in your hands at first) and, with your elbows supported, surround your ball of clay with your hands—straight in front of you.

Step 6. Squeeze: Basically you are squeezing in and pressing down at the same time. With a small soft ball of clay, this may happen almost by itself. Usually, it takes more time and more practice.

There are many methods of centering (and of working on the wheel), none of which is right or wrong. This is the method we use to teach students to center, and it almost always works the first or second time to their great surprise and satisfaction, having heard how impossible it is to center a ball of clay.

Think of your lump of clay as having three different planes or sides. When you squeeze, apply pressure:

• *In* with the finger tips of your right hand. If the clay were a clock, your right fingers, when surrounding the clay, would naturally fall at 12 o'clock or 1 o'clock. Squeeze the lump of clay with the tips of your right fingers to form the straight up and down base. See Figs. 2-3 and 2-4.

• *Down at a slant* with the heel of your left thumb. This will be directly opposite your right fingers, usually at six or seven o'clock. You have a lot of strength in this part of your hand, some of which comes

Fig. 2-3 Right-hand position for centering. Side view.

Fig. 2-4 Top view.

Fig. 2-5 Left-hand position for centering. Side view.

Fig. 2-6 Top view (potter's view).

from your arm and shoulder. See Figs. 2-5 and 2-6.

• And *straight down* over the top with the thumbs of one or both hands. All three of these pressures are applied simultaneously with your hands held right in front of you (and elbows anchored). The pressure/counterpressure squeeze of the right hand *in,* against the left hand pressing *down,* will almost always work. See Figs. 2-7 and 2-8. *Note:* If your hands are very

large or very small, try proportionally larger or smaller balls of clay at first.

In theory, you have three lines of force going toward the center of the wheel at different angles: The clay has no place to go but into the center.

Relax and think steady; do not force or overpower the clay. The clay moves gradually in a spiral manner; it doesn't just hop into the center.

If you are having trouble getting three

Fig. 2-7 Both hands centering. Side view.

Fig. 2-8 Top view.

distinct planes or getting your clay on center, here's the next thing to try.

• Squeeze the clay *in* with both hands harder than you press down with your thumbs. Let your clay grow up into a tall narrow column. Then do the reverse; press down from the top with your thumbs, and do no more than support the sides with your finger tips. In the process of making the clay grow taller and then flattening it out again, you may get the clay on center.

When your clay is centered, it feels "weightless," moving smoothly under your hands without wobbling. It should feel centered in all the succeeding steps of making the basic cylinder. If a tool or your finger is held lightly against the side of a centered piece of clay, it should continue to touch lightly on all sides as the wheel revolves. If it touches on one side and doesn't on the other, your clay isn't centered yet.

If you're having trouble, you or your teacher can usually tell what you're doing wrong by looking for the three planes mentioned earlier. If the bottom part of the lump is slanted way out and clay kind of merges with bat, you are not squeezing in enough with your right finger tips. (Sometimes just cleaning the extra "junk" clay off the edges of the bat—where your hand rides—will help.) If the top isn't straight across, you are probably not covering it with the flat edge of your thumb. If you have no slanted plane between the straight-up side and the straight-across top, you are not pushing the heel of your thumb in at an angle. The centered lump of clay doesn't have to have any set shape—this "picture" is just to let you know where you are or are not applying pressure and what your problem is if the clay is not centering for you.

One rule of teaching we follow is not to let students get too hung up over centering (as important as it is). If after trying for a while they still haven't centered their lump of clay, I put my hands over theirs and gently squeeze their hands over the clay until it is centered. This let's them feel how much pressure is required. In demonstrating, I've made it look so simple that the universal reaction is "Oh, you really do have to squeeze pretty hard, don't you." After everybody has their clay centered, we turn off the wheels for a minute and talk about what we're going to do next.

Opening. With your hands surrounding the clay as they were for centering, hold your thumbs together and aim the tips of your thumbs at the very center of the lump of clay. Press them down gradually until you form a hole in the lump. See Figs. 2–9 and 2–10. *Stop* within about half an inch of the bottom. If in doubt, leave the bottom a little thick—some clay stays on the wheel head when you string your pot to remove it, and a little heavier bottom gives the pot some support so the sides don't collapse when you take it off the wheel.

Just make a hole with your thumbs—don't try to widen the pot out yet. Make sure you haven't pushed your pot off center.

Forming the Floor of the Pot. Your right hand can stay in pretty much the same position as it was—surrounding the clay as for centering and opening, with this exception: Let your right thumb slide out of the hole and ride flat on the top rim, pressing down on it to keep the mass of clay centered as you move the walls out with your left hand.

Fig. 2-9 Opening. Side view.

Fig. 2-10 Top view.

Let your left hand hang limp in front of you and drop your fingers into the hole you just made in the center of the clay. See Figs. 2–11 and 2–12. The tip of your middle finger should touch the center point; your left thumb should fall outside the wall of clay (just under the heel of your right thumb, at about 4 o'clock on the circle).

To form a flat bottom, again apply pressure and counter pressure—*out* with your left middle finger and *down* with your right thumb. As you draw your middle finger out, give the clay time to spiral in front of your finger—you will see the spiral ridges in the clay, but they shouldn't be too extreme. Try to exert *even* pressure, so the floor is of uniform thickness from the center to the outside wall. *Do not* go past the diameter your original ball of clay was centered to. (If you want a wider pot, the lump of clay must be centered in a lower, wider shape in the first place.) See Figs. 2–13 and 2–14.

Fig. 2-11 Floor; left-hand position. Side view.

Fig. 2-12 Top view.

Fig. 2-13 Making the floor. Side view.

Fig. 2-14 Top view.

Coning. Coning is our term for the procedure involved in getting the clay into a slanted, almost volcano-looking shape—the diameter of the top considerably smaller than that of the base—in preparation for pulling up a cylinder. Invariably, if students are having trouble with their clay flaring out of control or always turning into low bowls when they are trying to pull straight cylinders, they have forgotten this preparatory step. It is very important to do this to counteract the natural pull of the wheel outward (centrifugal force). Coning can also be used to recenter the clay before starting each pull: If done with enough "down" pressure, it will insure solid, strong, level rims—not the uneven, thin rims that beginners tend to get.

How To Do It. Leave your hands the way they were for forming the bottom, but reverse pressures. While you were pulling *out* with your left middle finger toward your right thumb in the preceding step, push *in* with the side of your *left* thumb against the side of your left middle finger. Gradually, as the thumb rises up the side of the wall, push the wall of clay in towards

the center. See Figs. 2-15 and 2-16. Your left thumb should be parallel to the wheel head, and the whole side of the thumb, including the heel of your left hand, can rest on the wall of the pot, pushing in and sliding up. At the same time, you are applying counter pressure *down* with your right thumb (or your whole right hand with larger pieces of clay).

General Rule for Beginners. Keep the top rim narrower than the base. You will have more success controlling the clay. You can always pull the top out wider, but once it's flared out, it's very difficult to get it back in again.

Pulling Up the Walls. This requires new hand positions. (During these five separate steps, there are only three different hand positions.) Leave your left hand inside the pot with your middle finger at the base of the inside wall at about 4 o'clock, where it was when you finished making the floor and coning. Your left thumb will rest on top of your right thumb as a reference, once you get your right hand in position on the outside of the wall.

Fig. 2-15 Coning. Side view (showing position of left hand only).

Fig. 2-16 Top view (both hands).

Fig. 2-17 Hand positions for pulling the wall up. Side view.

Fig. 2-18 Top view.

To get your right hand into a good position for pulling: pick up a tool—say the needle or the wood digger tool—and hold it as if you were going to write with it. Remove it from your right hand, leaving your hand in the same cupped position with thumb against forefinger—tip of forefinger slightly extended. (Your fingers should re-

main *curved.*) Supporting your forefinger just down from the tip with your thumb, wet the tip of your forefinger and put it against the wall of clay at the base (4 o'clock) just opposite your left middle finger which is inside the pot. If the wall of clay weren't there, your two fingers would be squeezing against each other. See Figs. 2-17 and 2-18.

(Fingernails have to be short for this.) Let your left thumb fall on top of your right hand now.

A Sponge Might Help. If you are having a tendency to straighten your right forefinger out stiff, try holding the sponge cupped in your right hand as you work. This will force you to keep your hands curved. Also make sure that, as you work, your elbows (at least one of them) are anchored and that your left thumb keeps touching your right hand for stability—whenever possible. The more points of reference you have to your body, the steadier you will be.

Now you are ready to "pull." Get your wheel going at a medium slow speed (about 120 r.p.m.'s), slower than for centering and opening. Place your hands on the pot as described above, having wet the walls of your pot slightly beforehand. Squeeze the tips of your fingers together (right forefinger against left middle finger on inside of pot) until a ridge begins to form at the bottom of the wall. Slowly begin moving your fingers up the side of the pot, always remaining *under* the ridge. You are actually "pushing" this ridge up to the top of the pot. To reach the desired thinness, this step needs to be repeated *two or three times.* If you thin too much in one pull, you risk thinning the bottom half so much that it can't support the heavy ridge above it and tears or buckles as a result. If you play around too long, your clay gets soggy and tired. You should be applying more pressure to your squeeze when your fingers are near the bottom of the wall and gradually less pressure as they approach the top. By doing this, you will achieve walls of uniform thickness from top to bottom. Beginners' pots tend to have very thick bottom sections of walls and thin rims.

Fig. 2–19 Recentering after the pull. Top view.

It is also helpful to "recenter" the top rim after each pull. Hold your hands steady on the rim, almost as if for coning very lightly. See Fig. 2–19.

TOOLS

A needle (awl) has several uses. If your top rim is uneven or too thin, it can be sliced off by holding the tip of the needle against the wall of clay and gradually pressing in. When you feel the point of the needle with your left hand on the inside, lift up, and a ring of clay will come off in your hands. Then smooth off the rough edge at the top of the pot with wet fingers, sponge, or chamois. See Fig. 2–20.

A wood modeling tool is used prior to stringing your pot for removal from the bat. Hold the wooden tool as if it were a pencil that you were going to write with—in your right hand. Support your right hand with your left hand, because there is a tendency for the revolving pot to pull the tool into itself, leaving an unwanted gouge. Cut an angle at the base of your pot at

Fig. 2-20 Using chamois to smooth the top rim.

Fig. 2-21 Trimming off excess with a wood tool.

to put your fingers when you remove it from the bat (don't put them on the walls or your pot will squish in your hands). It also means your trimming job will be easier when the pot is leather hard.

A cut off string—we use fish line on two wood dowels. See Fig. 2-22. Hold this taut, pressing it down toward the bat. It has a tendency to ride up. Start on the far side of your pot and slowly pull the string toward you under the pot, continually pressing the string down and keeping it taut. This can be done on a small pot with the wheel rotating slowly or stationary.

If the pot is too soggy to keep its shape when removed from the wheel and set on the wareboard or is otherwise a disaster, throw it in the mush bucket of clay to go back through the pugmill. (We add some ball clay to stiffen it up when we repug it. This fine-particled clay has been removed in the working and reworking of the clay and remains in the bucket of water used in throwing.) If at all possible, though, try to work each piece through, at least through the trimming and handles

Fig. 2-22 Stringing to cut pot off bat.

about 45°, leading with the point of the wood tool and holding the edge parallel to the pot. Then clean away the excess clay. See Fig. 2-21. This angle at the bottom of your newly thrown pot will give you a place

stages. This is the only way to become accustomed to the techniques involved in trimming, texturing, applying handles, etc. If, after that point, you should decide that the work is not immortal and need not be bisque- or glaze-fired, it can be dried out thoroughly, broken up into pieces, and slaked back down. Clay can be reclaimed as long as it has not been bisque-fired.

At the end of the second lesson, each student should have one small pot, perhaps a potential sitting or hanging planter, to keep for trimming next week—either the one we work through in unison or one he does afterward on his own if there is time. Students sign the pots with the needle and leave them on their class's wareboard. Then we cover the pots with plastic to keep them partially wet until the next week's class.

LESSON **3**

Trimming and Leather-Hard Decoration

"Leather hard" is the stage clay passes through between the soft state it was in while the pot was being formed and the bone-dry stage it will eventually reach before being bisque fired. It is a very "workable" stage. The clay is still soft enough that it can be textured, carved, have handles or knobs applied, be trimmed, etc., without deforming under pressure, as would a freshly thrown pot, and without cracking or breaking as would a bone-dry pot. There are various stages within leather hard. At the beginning or softer stage, paddling, deforming, texturing, or carving work better. Later on, handles, knobs, trimming, and construction work better. Normally, depending on humidity, a pot will reach leather hard a few hours after having been thrown, unless it is deliberately held under plastic or in a damp box to prevent it from drying out. The rims of pots dry faster and reach leather hard before the rest of the pot. Once this has happened, the pot should be turned upside down to equalize its moisture content as it continues to dry.

MAKING SOME DECISIONS

When your pot reaches the leather-hard stage, it is time to make some decisions about what you want it to be when it's finished. Will it require one or more handles? Will you want to decorate it with textural changes? How do you want the base to look? There are three possibilities for trimming the bottom of the pot. It can sit flat on its bottom, as would a mug. It can be footed with a small pedestal carved into the bottom, as would a bowl or bottle, for example. Or it can be trimmed into a curve for hanging, as for a planter. Decide on the basic shape for the bottom, and, before you turn your pot upside down for trimming, observe both the thickness of the walls and the profile of the inside of the pot.

TRIMMING

The difference between a beginner pot that looks like a beginner pot and one that looks fairly proficient is the trimming. Once we've finished stressing trimming to our students, not only do their own pots show a marked improvement, but the students become much more selective about the craftsmanship in the pots they buy from others. Our secret to trimming success with beginners is in introducing to them a tool not normally used in pottery—Surform. This tool makes trimming a pot more like grating cheese. Rarely does it stick, drag, or chatter the way a normal trimming tool might if the clay were a little too soft.

Step 1: Centering the leather-hard pot (Fig. 3–1). Hold your elbows anchored in the same position as for centering a lump of clay for throwing. Put your leather-hard pot upside down on the bat. Start the wheel going slowly (slightly slower than for pulling a cylinder: 100–120 r.p.m.'s). Try to tap the pot into the center. The easiest way seems to be to let your left hand feel the pot on the left side and to tap the pot with short staccato taps with your right hand. As you feel the off-centeredness with your left hand, tap with your right hand. This is a matter of timing which you will gradually catch on to. It partially

depends on the speed of your reflexes and the speed at which the wheel is rotating. Trying to explain it is like trying to tell someone when to swing at a baseball—it's a matter of hand-eye coordination and a lot of practice.

(Note: A good way to practice this type of centering is to fill a one-pound coffee can half full of sand and try to tap it into the center of the wheel head.)

Step 2: Anchoring your pot to the wheel head (Fig. 3–2). Once you have centered your leather-hard pot upside down, stop

Fig. 3-1 Tapping a pot onto center.

Fig. 3-2 Anchoring a pot with three balls of clay.

the wheel. Take three small balls of clay and position them evenly at three points around your pot—setting them on the bat right beside the wall of the pot. Then press down on all three at once—toward the bat, not toward the pot. Start the wheel revolving slowly again. If the pot isn't anchored securely and comes loose, the wads of clay either weren't big enough or close enough to the wall of the pot. If you applied pressure unevenly to the balls of clay, you may discover that your pot has moved off center slightly. Stop the wheel, remove the pieces of clay, and start again. It is also helpful, unless the clay is particularly sticky, to dampen the bottom of the three wads slightly by rubbing them across a sponge before positioning them. This will help insure that your pot stays anchored securely as you work on it.

A word of caution: When you remove the little balls of clay, especially if your pot has a flared-out rim, be careful to remove them one-by-one *before* you lift the pot off the bat. Otherwise, the rim may remain under the ball of clay, and a whole chunk of it will crack off.

Step 3: Using the trimming tools. Start the wheel again. Hold trimming tools with your hand over the top of the handle—unlike a pencil. You will then automatically be pressing down somewhat on them. Hold the Surform as shown in Fig. 3–3. In both cases you need to have both hands on the tool—with one finger riding on center (or on the outside rim of the foot once it's established) for a reference point.

Use the Surform tool (Fig. 3–3) first to flatten the bottom and smooth out any roughness or unevenness in the clay. With Surform, the wheel can be going slightly faster (120–140 r.p.m.'s). If you are leaving the bottom rounded, as for a

Fig. 3–3 Inge trimming with Surform tool.

hanging planter, the Surform may be the only tool you will need to use (Fig. 3–4). If you are leaving a flat bottom and straight sides as in the case of a mug, jar, or cylinder, you may want to "pop" the center of the bottom in with a quick tap so that the bottom is concave and sits firmly on a table without wobbling. Again the Surform may be the only tool you need for smoothing out the bottom and lower sides. If you want to make a foot on your pot, other trimming tools will be required.

Step 4: Making a foot. Many pots, like bowls and bottles, look better if they sit on a foot. A foot elevates the pot visually and makes it look less heavy by giving it a small pedestal to sit on at the base.

• Take a regular trimming tool (the shape doesn't matter too much) and establish the *outside* of the foot—carving straight down with the point of the tool (Fig. 3-5). Then trim off the excess clay and shape the outside wall (remembering the inside profile), blending it in an even curve into the foot (Fig. 3-6). Once you have established the outside of the foot, do not disturb it—otherwise, you'll keep moving it farther and farther toward the center, making the finished pot unstable.

• Once the outside of the foot is established, let your right fourth finger ride on it as a guide. Then, cut down parallel to it, about half an inch in from it, to establish the inside of the rim.

• After the inside of the foot has been established, start with the point of your trimming tool in the center of the pot and carve out the clay inside the rim. You may need to use both the point and the flat edge of the trimming tool to finally achieve a neat recessed area inside the foot rim (Fig. 3-7).

Fig. 3-4 The bottom of a hanging pot trimmed into a curve.

Fig. 3-5 Setting the outside edge of a foot with the trimming tool.

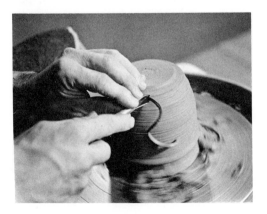

Fig. 3-6 Trimming away excess clay to shape contour.

Fig. 3-7 Trimming away clay inside foot.

Tips on Trimming. If clay is the right consistency for trimming, it will peel off through the trimming tool like a potato peel. If the clay is too soft, the trimming tool will tend to stick and catch. If the clay is too dry, the tool will just scrape along over the surface of the pot. The better a job you did stringing your pot off the wheel, the easier your trimming job will be. You will discover that if your top rim was uneven after throwing, you will be trying to trim a wobbly pot. If this is the case, try to level it by putting a small piece of soft clay under the low spot in the rim.

Finishing. Trimming produces a texture that is coarser than that of throwing. If the clay is quite heavily grogged, you will get a porous open texture, as opposed to the spiral finger marks above it. The pot can be deliberately left with this coarse texture, or you can carry the throwing lines all the way down the sides of the pot by running a sponge over it followed by a finger tip. When the pot is finished, it should look unified—not as if you threw part of it and then trimmed the other half, starting and stopping somewhere in the middle (Fig. 3–8).

Fig. 3–8 Cross section of curved and footed pots.

Note: For anchoring and trimming irregular shapes, such as bottles and lids, see Lesson 7.

Students begin to realize that it takes as long or longer to trim a pot as it does to throw one. We remind them that many pots require handles and decorating at this stage as well. Then, they begin to realize why we keep claiming that in our production studio, we spend no more than ten percent of our total time throwing. There is a great deal more involved.

LEATHER-HARD DECORATING

Once you've trimmed your pot, it's time to decide whether you would like to decorate it at the leather-hard stage. (Other types of decorating can be done later on after bisque-firing.) By now, you should have a good idea of how you want your pot to look when it's finished. In working with clay, it is important to *plan ahead.* Certain things can only be done at particular stages. (See chart). Leather hard is the time to decide whether you want to attach a handle, whether you want to put holes in your pot so you can hang it, whether you want to decorate it texturally by carving or impressing a design into it, or even whether you want to add a contrasting clay color decoratively. If, on the other hand, you want to work with glazes and stains decoratively, this should wait until after the pot has been bisque-fired. Some techniques, even, will need to be initiated at the leather-hard stage and completed after bisque-firing. The possible combinations of effects are infinite and ever-challenging.

Don't Over-Do It. When presented with so many decorating possibilities, it may be a

STAGES OF CLAY: A POT FROM START TO FINISH

1. *Soft Clay*
   Wedge
   Shape the basic pot (wheel or handbuilding)
   Cut off the bat neatly to aid trimming
   Leave finger marks on smooth sides as decoration
   Leave bottom thick if footing later on
   Certain deformations (pitcher spout) can be made at this stage

2. *Set-up Clay: Soft-Leather Hard*
   Paddling for flattening sides (Fig. 3–9)
   Carving as for lanterns (Fig. 3–10)

3. *Leather Hard*
   Trimming (signing with pointed tool)
   Decorating that requires texturing, incising, additions of clay
   Application of colored engobes
   Addition of handles
   Making holes for planters, lamps etc.; cutting out clock bodies
   Addition of knobs or handles on lids after trimming
   Construction of complex pots, thrown or handbuilt

4. *Bone Dry (sanding roughness before bisque firing—FRAGILE)*

5. *Bisqued Pots (thrown or handbuilt)*
   Waxing—functional and decorative
   Applying stain—especially to highlight textures
   Applying glaze

6. *Fired Pots*
   Add final parts—corks, leather, lamp parts, mirror glass, bamboo handles, etc. Grind bottoms for any kilnwash. Critique firing and plan for changes. Display nicely. (Enjoy.)

Fig. 3-9 Paddling a pot to change its shape.

Fig. 3-10 Carving a lantern, authors' design.

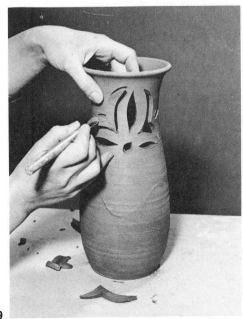

temptation to try a little of everything on the same pot. It is best to stick to one idea at a time. Keep in mind that clay is a natural material, and often simplicity is very effective. A nice simple form with a rich glaze may need no further decoration. Finger marks from throwing, contrasted with a smooth area for a rim, may simply need to be accentuated by a second coat of glaze. On a simple mug, this is often enough.

Be Appropriate.

• A finished pot can and should show some of the elements of how it was made. Soft clay acquires texture as you are working with it—throwing marks, construction marks, even glazing marks. Don't try to "erase" these and redecorate; incorporate them.

• Some tools and materials used in decorating are more appropriate for certain effects than others. Very sharp detail can be achieved by incising with pointed objects at the leather-hard stage or by brushing detailed patterns on with wax or stain after the pot has been bisque-fired. On the other hand, engobe treatments may work better with more general, freer brush strokes and patterns, as some of the detail may be lost once it is covered by a glaze. Knowing how to use tools and materials appropriately for the desired effect takes judgment that can only be developed with practice and experience.

• Some decorating techniques are more appropriate than others in the case of functional pots. Bowls cannot have a rough sculptural surface on the inside, pitchers must have spouts and handles which function properly, etc. If it is to be a functional pot, keep this in mind as you decorate.

• The overall effect of the finished pot is important. If you have thrown an interesting form, you probably will want to decorate simply to enhance the form. If, on the other hand, you prefer to concentrate on the decorating and make that the focal point of your pot, throw a plain form which will act as a canvas to receive your artwork. Don't make the pot so complex that form, decoration, and glaze are all in competition with each other.

Capitalize on Your Mistakes. Be flexible. Lots of our students do very creative incising to cover up a place on the pot that was nicked earlier—usually when they were trying to center the pot for trimming, got their wheel going too fast, and had the pot fly off the wheel. Accept the fact that some decisions are made for you and that you may have to change plans in midstream. This is how discoveries are made.

A word of caution: the rims of leather-hard pots become more fragile as they continue to dry. Because of this and because beginner pots tend to have thin, weak rims besides, students should avoid picking their pots up by the rims. They may break right off. Learn to handle pots with two hands at the base; and whenever pressing to apply handles or decoration, support the inside of the pot as well. Avoid adding clay to the very top part of the pot whenever possible and you will run less risk of cracking the rim.

MATERIALS FOR LEATHER-HARD DECORATION

Here is a list of possible materials you can use for decorating at the leather-hard stage. Feel free to improvise as well.

1. Engobes of different-colored slip clay —one darker and one lighter than your clay body, perhaps. The easiest way to make an engobe is to take some sloppy clay that is being slaked down for reclaiming; stir and screen it until it is about the consistency of a thick glaze; then add coloring oxides. If your throwing body is quite dark by itself, you may need to mix up an engobe from scratch. This will be basically the same as your clay body but with less colorant in it. (*Note:* although the word "engobe" originally had a slightly different meaning because of its French origin, it tends to be used synonymously with "colored-slip" clay, and that is how we are using it here.)

2. Brushes for applying the engobes— a 1½"-wide paint brush and some finer bamboo-type brushes.

3. Wax to use under engobes in resist patterns; these are usually brushed on.

4. Other applicators, such as an ear syringe for slip trailing fine-lined designs or a baster (the kind you use for roasting a turkey) for very coarse textural applications of engobe (Fig. 3–11).

5. Objects for texturing the clay:

• Pointed objects, such as a needle tool, a wood digger tool, and a trimming tool, will enable you to carve lines of varying thickness. A hacksaw blade is good for "combing" patterns.

• Stamps: Many potters make their own stamps by rolling out a small piece of clay and flattening one end, then carving a design into the flat end, letting it dry, and firing it. You can make any type of geometric pattern you like this way. Stamps can be carved out of wood or plaster as well, or found already made. Just look around.

• Natural objects for texture. Pine cones, corn cobs, sea shells, nut shells,

Fig. 3–11 Slip-trailed test piece (ear syringe).

leaves, grasses, etc., can all be pressed into soft clay to leave a textural pattern.

We keep a few sample pots around to give our students ideas. That way they can see how various techniques work before experimenting on their own pots.

PROCEEDING WITH THE LEATHER-HARD DECORATION

Decorating a pot at the leather-hard stage is a matter of either changing the surface of the clay—by adding on or taking away clay—and/or changing the color of the clay by adding engobes. Either the surface or the color can be changed individually, or the two can be done in conjunction with each other.

Adding a constrasting clay color is done by means of applying an engobe. There are a number of ways of doing this.

1. If you have a large bucket full of engobe, you can dip your pot in it just as if you were glazing a bisque-fired pot. (It

should be about the thickness of heavy cream.) Be careful, if your pot absorbs too much water it will become soft again—handle gingerly.

2. If you are working from small containers or want only a partial application of contrasting color, try "banding" your pot. Recenter your pot as if for trimming (or leave it there when you have finished trimming). Hold a wide-bristle paint brush dipped in engobe (fairly thick engobe is best for this) flat against the pot as it revolves on the wheel; continue until you have coated the pot with an even band of engobe; repeat if you want.

3. Brush engobe on with bamboo brushes in broad free decorative patterns. Or: Brush the patterns on with wax resist; let dry; then brush (or dip) engobe over the pot. Where it is waxed, the original clay color will remain. The engobe will only sink into the nonwaxed areas. (Paper cutout forms can also be used as resists.)

4. Slip trail engobe with either the ear syringe or baster. You will get both a color and a textural change with this.

Texture—Incising, Sgraffito, and Mishima.
There are various techniques for adding texture to a pot. If you carve a design into the soft clay it is called *incising*. If you had applied engobe and let it dry beforehand, this same carving would be called *sgraffito,* a popular Italian decorating technique. If you had carved the design first and then inlaid it with slip afterward, it would be called *mishima.* Incising, then, can be done alone or in combination with engobes.

Impressing an object into the clay will also texture the surface. Stamps or natural objects can be used alone or combined with contrasting engobes, for textural effects.

Fig. 3-12 Balls of clay added and stamped.

Fig. 3-13 Paddled balls of clay on contrasting background.

Fig. 3-14 Clay roughly added and scratched through.

Fig. 3-15 Vase; Gerry Williams. Copper and manganese slip, sgraffito with white matt glaze. (*Courtesy Jean Delius*)

Fig. 3-16 Lamp; Pat Probst Gilman. Hand-thrown porcelain with incised decoration, clear glaze.

Fig. 3-17 Stoneware thrown form; Vivika and Otto Heino. Sides pushed out, contrasting engobe panel with black engobe brush strokes, interior glazed only.

These texturing techniques can be used on handbuilt pots as well. Impressing patterns and textures is actually easier with slabs than with leather-hard thrown pots. Not only are the slabs softer, they are flat on a counter top and can't collapse.

In the case of a thrown pot, impressing is sometimes easier if you add on a soft ball of clay first (cross hatch and slip first) and then press the stamp or found object into the fresh clay (*supporting* the pot from behind). See Fig. 3–12. This is an easy decorating technique that the children often try, but usually one or two get pots with rim cracks from over-exuberant pressing.

Adding Clay On. The above is really an example of adding clay on as well as impressing. Instead of stamping the ball of clay you have added on, you can add quite a few balls and coils randomly (don't forget to score and slip, otherwise they will come off). To flatten the balls out, cover them with burlap, and paddle them, leaving the burlap texture on the flattened forms. This works very well if you have applied engobe first to give a contrasting background to the paddled additions of clay (see Fig. 3–13).

Bits of clay can be added roughly by pressing and dragging your finger. This will give a very rough sculptural surface or pattern to the wall of your pot (see Fig. 3–14).

Forms can be modeled and added at this stage, or elaborate handles can be used decoratively or functionally and added at this stage. Handles are the subject of the next lesson. (Hopefully we haven't spent so much time decorating and trimming this week that we haven't been able to throw a pot to add a handle to the next week.)

Figures 3–15 through 3–17 show pots decorated primarily at leather-hard.

LESSON **4**

Pulling and Attaching a Handle

In this lesson you will learn to pull handles and attach them to your leather-hard pot. This is a separate but very necessary skill which will require practice to perfect.

PREPARING THE CLAY

1. Wedge up some clay (on the soft side) as you would for throwing. Instead of patting it into a ball, roll it slightly on the wedging table (the way you would make a thick coil for coiling a pot) so that you have a tapered, oblong piece of clay. You should be able to grasp the fat end easily in your left hand; the other end can taper down almost to a point.

2. Get a pan of water and sit at a table (or at your wheel) with the water directly in front of you. Hold the clay straight up and down when pulling the handle—arms per-

pendicular to your body and supported on your knees (or ribs) as if for throwing.

3. Don't wet your left hand; if it's slippery you can't hang on to the lump of clay you're pulling your handle from. Keep the right hand *good and wet* (it's almost impossible to get the clay too wet at this stage). There should be no drag or friction as your right hand slides down the handle.

4. Check the size of your pot and think appropriately. Plan to do the handle in two steps: First a cylindrical tube and then a flattened handle.

MAKING A CYLINDRICAL TUBE

Hold your right hand in a relaxed curved position and make a circle between your thumb and forefinger; let your right thumb rest on top of your right forefinger (Fig. 4–1). As your hand slides down the tube of clay (clay resting in the fork between thumb and forefinger), you will close down the size of this circle—gradually thinning the tube of clay but keeping it round.

Don't Squeeze the Clay; Slide Down It. See Fig. 4–2. No lumps or thin spots should develop. If they do, break it off and start again. You are trying to form a solid clay tube about four inches long and one inch in diameter (for a mug).

If you have a tendency to thin more in the middle of the handle, you should work at thinning just the bottom section first; then move up a little and work from the middle down to the tip; then gradually move up to the fat part and take long strokes all the way from top to bottom.

FLATTENING THE HANDLE

1. Once you have a round tube slightly fatter at the top than the bottom, start flattening it out with your right thumb. (See Figs. 4–3 and 4–4.) Hold the side of your right forefinger behind the handle as a support; hold your right thumb at *right angles* to the handle and your forefinger so that the *tip* of your thumb (not the first joint) slides down the clay, flattening it out and forming an indentation. Occasionally you will have to turn the handle over and repeat this on the other side. And also occasionally, especially if the handle starts to get too wide or the edges too thin, run your thumb and forefinger along the edges to round them up and squeeze them in a little narrower. (See Fig. 4–5.)

2. When you're done, the completed handle should have even, rounded, not-too-thin edges, and a regular, not-too-deep

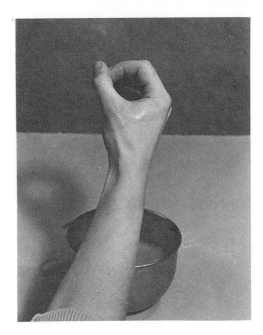

Fig. 4–1 Hand position for pulling a handle.

Fig. 4–2 Forming the "tube."

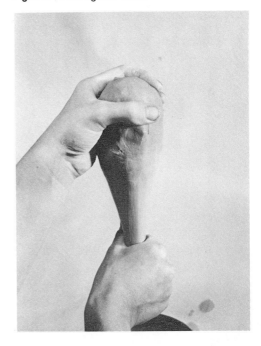

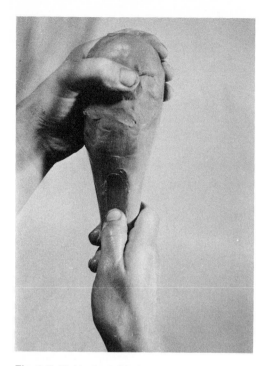

Fig. 4-3 Flattening with thumb.

Fig. 4-4 Side view of thumb pulling handle.

Fig. 4-5 Smoothing edges.

Fig. 4-6 Ready to break off at top.

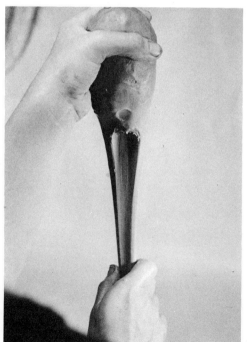

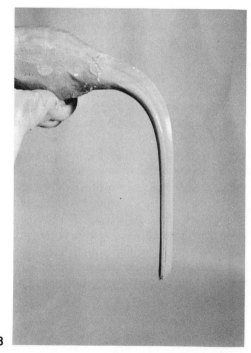

indentation where your thumb was pulling the clay down the handle. It is better to concentrate on evenness rather than try to get the handle super-thin. (See Fig. 4–6.)

Pinch off the handle at the top. We usually lay the handles on their sides in a curve on the wareboard (not on plaster—they stick). If, in a two-hour class, we do handles at the beginning of the class, then trim the mug or pitcher they will be attached to, and then work some more on the wheels, by the time we are ready to attach the handles (the last ten or fifteen minutes of class), they have set-up adequately. They need to be dry enough to retain their shape and not slump when attached to the mug—but not so dry as to be brittle. The closer the handle and mug body are to the same stage of wetness, the better the handle will adhere.

ATTACHING THE HANDLE

Take the needle tool; score (cross-hatch) the mug top and bottom where you want to attach the handle. If the rim is at all brittle, score the mug at least ½ an inch down from the top. See Fig. 4–7. Add slip.

Caution. Support the inside of the wall you are pressing the handle onto. This is another leather-hard disaster lesson that is often learned the hard way—once the pot has cracked, there's no mending it.

Sometimes you wish you had a third hand for this. Hold one hand (except for the thumb) inside the mug, against the back of the wall you are attaching the handle to. See Fig. 4–8. Hold the *curve* of your handle in the other hand, supporting it underneath. Keep your eye on the curve to see if it starts to develop little hairline

Fig. 4-7 Cross-hatching or scoring before adding slip.

Fig. 4-8 Attaching handle to top of pitcher, directly opposite spout.

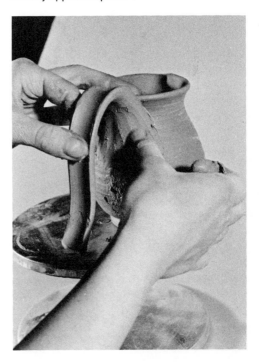

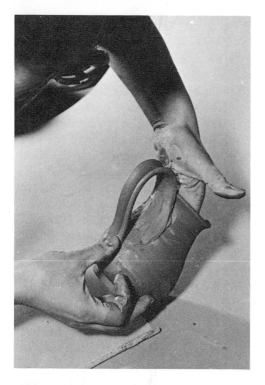

Fig. 4-9 Attaching bottom of handle.

Fig. 4-10 Stamping decoration.

cracks as you're working with it. If it has dried out a little too much, dab some water on it with a finger.

To apply, hold the fat end of the handle against the top of the mug where you have scored and added slip. With your other thumb work the clay smoothly into the surface of the mug. See Fig. 4-9. Then attach the bottom (*straight* underneath the top); and if you want, use a stamp for texture here. See Fig. 4-10. *Support* from behind.

Look at the profile of the mug and check the curve of the handle; it should be gentle, not abrupt—smooth, not wobbly or lumpy. Is it proportional to the pot? Will you be able to hold onto it and eventually drink (or pour) from the pot? (Don't try lifting by the handle now! Or at bone-dry.)

WHY BOTHER?

When I first tried to pull a handle, I immediately decided that the only answer was to roll out a slab of clay and cut a strip the right size for a handle. Why not? For two reasons:

Visually it always looks crude; it never has the smooth edges or natural taper of a pulled handle. More important, it isn't as strong. In pulling a handle, you are aligning particles of clay in a parallel orientation. This gives the handle infinitely more strength than a slab handle would have with its more randomly oriented clay particles.

So, even if you think it's ridiculous, frustrating, and not worth the bother, persist. It's worth perfecting. (See Fig. 4-11.) If you can't bear to just practice, use your "handles" to make napkin rings or a link chain. You'll get it. (And if all else fails, maybe you can trade somebody trimming for handles—that's what *we* do in our production.)

Figures 4-12 and 4-13 show a variety of pots with handles from which you may get an idea to start with.

Fig. 4-11 Students learning to pull handles.

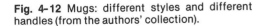

Fig. 4-12 Mugs: different styles and different handles (from the authors' collection).

Fig. 4-13 Stoneware pitcher; Carl Sande.

LESSON **5**

Review

This is usually the week that our students show up gasping for breath. So we slow down and go back over the basics, concentrating on problem areas and going a little farther into "shaping" the cylinder.

Following are checklists for the most common problems our beginners have.

GENERAL

1. Are you doing *five* different steps? Center, open, make the floor, "cone" into a volcano, pull. Are your hands in the right positions for each step?

2. When you apply pressure, are you also applying counter-pressure?

3. Are you keeping your arm anchored —not up in the air or floating around the pot? *Do not* follow the pot (counterclockwise) around the wheel—work in one place.

CENTERING

1. Are you removing your hands too fast? Some students have the clay basically centered then whisk their hands off with a great flourish, throwing the clay off center again. *Release* the pressure first. *Then remove* your hands slowly. (This applies to pulling as well.)

2. Are you getting three distinct planes . . . showing that you are applying pressure in three directions? Is your right hand squeezing opposite and against your left hand (pressure/counterpressure)?

3. Do you have too much junk on your bat or wheel head? Take the digger tool, trim a neat line at the bottom of the lump you are centering and then clean all extraneous messy clay off. This trick usually helps a lot.

4. Is your wheel going fast enough? You need a certain amount of speed for

centering. Beginners make the mistake of thinking if they go slower they'll have more control. (*Caution:* With the electric wheel, it's also possible to go too fast—with the kick wheel it isn't. We usually switch the speed-freaks to the kick wheel for a while to see if that helps.)

5. Are you keeping your hands and the clay wet enough? Drag will make centering difficult. (You may even feel the clay getting warm from the friction.)

6. Are you giving the clay time to move? Use slow steady pressure so the clay can spiral *itself* into the center—it doesn't hop in the way a leather-hard pot does for trimming.

7. After you center, open, and make a floor, are you really getting a good volcano-shaped cone? Usually if you are having trouble pulling a cylinder, the problem occurred earlier on, in the preparatory stages.

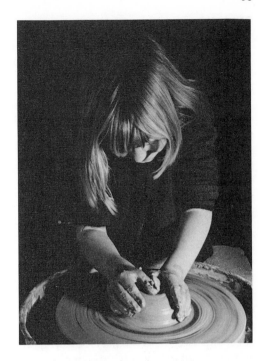

Fig. 5-1 Inge Wettlaufer (age 7) centering.

Fig. 5-2 Coning.

Fig. 5-3 Pulling.

PULLING

1. Is the clay peeling off in front of your forefinger half way up a pull? Are you tending to try to pull with straight fingers?

Try holding a sponge in your cupped right palm. This will keep your hand in a natural curve. If you hold a piece of the sponge under your forefinger where it touches the pot, this will tend to lubricate the pot more evenly. Many students try throwing with the sponge in their hand at this point—it does help.

2. Are you getting the even, distinct, spiral lines up the side of your pot that you want, or does it look like you "mushed" the walls instead of pulling them? Make sure you are forming a definite ridge at the bottom of the wall and staying under it all the way up. It's easy to let your finger get pulled up over it. You may be trying to pull the cylinder up too fast—move your hands very gradually upward . . . the spiraling takes a while.

3. Is your wall tearing and coming apart halfway up? Rewet the walls; the friction may be causing it to tear. Decrease some pressure as your hands go up the pot. The top half tends to be thinner than the bottom half and requires less squeezing.

4. Does your cylinder keep getting narrower and narrower with each pull? Are you having trouble getting the clay up out of the bottom? You probably are pushing in too hard with your right forefinger. Squeeze *out* from the inside *equally* with your left middle finger. To pull a straight cylinder, you need *equal* squeezing pressure from both hands.

Fig. 5-4 Contemplating her finished pot.

Fig. 5-5 Kurt Wettlaufer (age 5½) preparing a ball of clay.

5. Does your pot keep flaring out? As you pull up, think that you are moving both hands *in* toward the center somewhat. Also, recone the top after each pull (this will push the rim toward the center and also recenter the clay). Are you pushing in too much in the middle of the wall causing the top to flare out? Are you pulling with your wheel going too *fast*? Slow down after opening and coning. Centrifugal force operating on soft clay naturally produces a flare. (Center at 180 rpms and pull or trim at 120 rpms or less—approximately.)

Comment: When things start going from bad to worse, take a break for a minute. You tend to start fighting the clay, getting tense and aggravating both your coordination and the timing. Do some deep breathing and calm down before you tackle the clay again. *Relax.*

NEW SHAPES

Throwing a Cylinder with More Shape to It —A Rounded Pitcher or Cork Jar. This is both a review of the basics involved in pulling a cylinder and an introduction to the next lesson on lids. It requires a little more control—both in shaping the pot and in producing a top rim which is fairly constricted and absolutely round. The rim must also be level and, in the case of the cork jar, a specific size.

Shaping a Curve.

1. Take a slightly larger ball of clay. Center, open, make a floor and cone, preliminary to pulling.

2. In pulling a cylinder with more of a curve to it, the first two pulls for thinning should be pretty straight up—wait until the

Fig. 5-6 Centering.

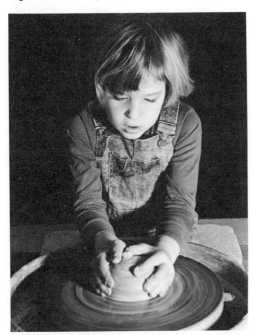

Fig. 5-7 Pulling.

last pull to put the curve in, and then leave it. A curve "sogs" much more readily than a straight wall.

Try to keep the top of the pot narrower than the bottom—work in under the rim with your left hand; don't let the top rim flare out—it's hard to get it back in.

3. Let the relationship of your squeezing fingers change slightly—from almost directly opposite each other to higher or lower depending on whether you are pushing the clay out or in.

To round the curve out, the left hand is higher than the right hand. Think of your right forefinger as a fulcrum—with the left hand pushing out over it.

To bring the curve back in (provided the rim was left narrow), reverse the positions—the left middle finger acting as the fulcrum, the right hand moving up over it and pushing the wall of clay in toward the center.

This type of curving requires practice for good results; it is similar whether making pitchers, bottles, or even closed forms.

Making a Pitcher. To form the pouring spout, *stop* the wheel. Support the rim of the pot with your left forefinger and thumb in an upside down U (like a croquet wicket). You can pull the lip with your right forefinger, through the "wicket." Pull gradually with easy strokes. (If the rim is very soft from overworking, the pouring spout may tend to crack or buckle.) Make sure you start your spout far enough down (the inside of the pot) so you form a good channel for the liquid. (See Fig. 4-13.)

Making a Cork Stopper Jar. Everybody knows now about *shrinkage* in drying (and will shortly discover that it continues on firing). The pot the students thought was so big the night they threw it looks miniscule, hardly worth owning up to the next week. If a cork is going to fit once the pot is fired, the wet pot has to be thrown larger.

Shrinkage depends on the amount of fine-particled clay in the body and the temperature you fire to. Our clay body fired to cone 10 shrinks: 5% from wet to dry, 1% from dry to bisque-fired, and 5% from bisque- to glaze-fired, or about 11% total linear shrinkage.

Our method for fitting the pot to the cork is as follows: Hold the cork upside down. If the widest part of the cork will just fit through the opening of the jar you are throwing, it should fit correctly, right-side-up, after the pot has been fired. (See Fig. 6–2.)

There is some variation here. If you have had to widen the mouth of the jar to achieve the final width, the pot will tend to shrink *in* more, trying to go back to its former width. If you have had to push the clay *in* slightly to get the rim to the right size, the fired pot will tend to shrink a little less. Clay has a certain amount of "memory" and will, on drying, go back to an earlier shape (this movement is very slight and rarely noticeable except in this instance when you are trying for an exact fit with a nonceramic material).

As an aid, flare the rim of the jar out slightly. If there is a taper, the cork has a better chance of fitting.

LESSON 6

Covered
Jars

The next thing you need to know after throwing and trimming cylinders and pulling and attaching handles is how to make a lid that fits. Inspect some covered jars carefully before trying it. Lift the lids and notice the various ways of seating them. (See Fig. 6-1.)

THE STOPPERED JAR

The easiest kind of jar to make for a lid is really just a cylinder, which can receive a cork, as described in Lesson 5, or a thrown stopper-style lid. The cylinder can be any shape but must be on center and level at the rim. If you are going to throw a stopper-style lid, we suggest that you not make the

opening of the cylinder too wide. (See Figs. 6-2 and 6-3.) Otherwise, you will have to attach a knob or handle in a third step after trimming the lid. The knob, especially, is difficult for a beginner.

The stopper-type lid that fits the plain jar is thrown *upside down,* either off the bat or off the hump (see Fig. 6-4). As long as you work with a piece of clay that is large enough, you can use whatever size lump is easiest for you to center.

As you work, proceed through centering and opening as usual with the exception that your thumbs only need to press down a shallow opening (½ in.). Put your left middle finger in this small opening as you normally do to make the floor of a pot, but instead of having your left thumb rest way out on the edge of the lump of clay, let it ride up half an inch and squeeze in a little; this will form the ridge that sits on the top rim of the jar.

Chapter opening art: Stoneware lidded jar; Alan Caiger-Smith, Great Britain. Tawny-orange luster, 15″ high, brush decoration on the glaze.

Fig. 6-1 The authors' canister "set"; stoneware covered jars by graduate students from Alfred.

Fig. 6-2 Measuring for fit with upside-down cork.

The hole in the center of your lid should be deeper than the outside edge (where your thumb is resting). If you intend to trim a curve into the lid later on, make a curved floor—deeper in the center and curving up to the height of the outside edge.

Measure with calipers (1) the inside diameter of the jar rim (Fig. 6–5), which should be a little larger than (2) the outside diameter of the walls of the stopper lid.

Fig. 6-3 Throwing jar with straight-up rim for stopper-type lid.

Fig. 6-4 Throwing the lid.

Fig. 6-5 Measuring pot inside to see if lid will fit.

61

Fig. 6-6 Throwing a ginger jar.

Fig. 6-7 Measuring the ginger jar lid to fit over the top rim.

THE GINGER JAR

The ginger jar is a variation of the stoppered jar. The lid of the ginger jar, instead of fitting inside the opening, fits *over* the top rim (Fig. 6-6)—like an upside-down shallow bowl. The jar is similar to the stoppered jar, with the top rim straight up, but it is pushed in at least an inch narrower than the body of the jar, leaving a shelf for the inverted bowl-lid to sit on.

The lid, again, can be thrown off a hump of clay or flat off the bat, depending on what size piece of clay is easiest for you to work with.

Measure with calipers (1) the outside of the jar rim, which should be a little smaller than (2) the inside of the rim of the bowl-lid (Fig. 6-7).

THE FLANGE JAR
WITH THE KNOB LID

The most difficult jar for beginners to make appears to be the one with the flange in the rim to hold the flat lid. We have the students put the flange in right after they have finished coning the clay—with pressure down on the top rim from the left forefinger "splitting" the top rim in half, the inside half lower and "grooved" to receive the lid (Fig. 6-8). However, this

Fig. 6-8 Flange-style jar; establishing the flange early.

tends to get in the way as you are pulling the cylinder up. But if you wait until after you have pulled the cylinder to put the flange in (Fig. 6–9), you have two problems —usually the wall is soggy and buckles under the "down" pressure to the rim. And if the top rim isn't fat enough, there isn't enough clay left to press down into the flange. So it's best to get the flange at least established before beginning to thin the walls.

The lid for this most difficult of jars is, perhaps, the easiest and most fun kind to make. The easiest is a flat lid with a knob, although a recessed lid with a knob can also be made to fit the same flange, as can a curved convex lid.

To make the flat lid with the knob, center the clay. Then, press both thumbs down, *either side* of center, leaving a "knob" of clay higher up in the center as you flatten down the outside part of the lump with your thumbs. Treat the flat lid as if you were making the floor of a pot without walls, pressing down beside the knob with your left middle finger and drawing it out to 4 o'clock, controlling the outside rim with down pressure from your

right hand. (This lid is made "right-side-up.")

Measure with calipers (1) the inside of the top rim of the jar and (2) the outside of the flat lid.

Establish the thickness of your lid first. When you have the lid drawn out to the proper thickness, take the wooden digger tool, cut a ring at about the right diameter (Fig. 6–10), remove the excess clay, smooth up the trimmed edge, and measure again. If the lid is a little too wide, you can just press in a bit to decrease its diameter.

When you have the flat part of the lid the diameter and the thickness that you want, go back and work on the lump you left in the center for a knob. Shape this as if it were a miniature pot you are throwing. Pull it up, flare it out, round it into a closed form (leaving a little hole), etc. *But,* check your pot to make sure the style lid you're making is appropriate to the style of the jar. Also remember that, functionally, a knob is to be grasped. You should be able to get your fingers under it and get a good grip on it when you are removing lid from jar later on in use. (See Fig. 6–11.)

Fig. 6–9 Finishing the flange jar.

Fig. 6–10 Flat knob lid for flange-style jar.

Fig. 6-11 Recessed lid for flange-style jar.

Fig. 6-12 Covered jar; Robin Hopper, Canada. Faceted and agate porcelain, interior glazed only. (*Courtesy Jean Delius*)

ERRORS IN MEASURING

If you are going to err:

1. with stopper type lids, make the stopper walls a little too *narrow* in diameter.

2. with ginger jar lids, make the diameter of the lid too *wide*.

3. with flat or recessed lids for a flange jar, make the lid diameter a little too *wide*; it's not hard to trim back, but impossible to enlarge.

In our own lessons, the rest of this class is devoted to "free throw." This is the last class for throwing if we are to be able to process all pots for glazing by the last class. It is usually this weekend also that we have our raku firing. Everybody has pinched a few pots and brought them back to be bisque-fired prior to the happening. (See Section III, p. 158.)

Figures 6–12 through 6–18 show covered jars done by different artists.

Fig. 6-13 Stoneware covered jar; Bob Woo. Faceted, oxide stamps and brushwork.

Fig. 6-14 Stoneware tea caddy; Mary Nyberg. Ginger jar lid over insert. (*Courtesy Jean Delius*)

Fig. 6-15 Stoneware covered jar; Carl Sande.

Fig. 6-16 Stoneware canister set; George and Nancy Wettlaufer. Wax resist, border design.

Fig. 6-17 Stoneware mustard jar; Ruth McKinley, Canada, 1973. Wooden spreader by D. L. McKinley. Slipped outside with porcelain clay, cone 9 reduction, wood-fired. (*Courtesy Jean Delius*)

Fig. 6–18 Covered jar; Robert Turner.
(Photo by Linn Underhill)

LESSON **7**

Teapots

TEAPOTS

A teapot is a covered jar to which a spout and handle have been attached. Teapots are really the ultimate challenge in wheel-thrown pottery because they require control over all disciplines: shaping the pot, fitting a lid to it, trimming both appropriately, throwing and carving a narrow spout, and pulling and attaching a handle. Almost every potter sooner or later develops his own style teapot.

We have talked about forming and trimming a jar and lid. For a teapot, a somewhat squatty shape is better than a tall, thin covered jar. The spout should be thrown at the same time as the jar and the lid so that it is in the leather-hard stage when construction begins. A spout can best be thought of as the neck of a bottle, although it should not flare back out much at the end. A good spout that pours well takes much experimenting and practice. Basically, the liquid should not be constricted too rapidly or you may get "chugging" when you pour rather than a steady, curved stream. The edge of the spout should be quite sharp so it will cut off the flow of liquid without an extra "drip." For this reason, some people wipe glaze from the bottom edge of the spout before firing it. Look at some of the shapes of spouts in the teapot photographs at the end of the chapter.

Before beginning work on the leather-hard pieces (jar, lid, and spout), pull your handle so it can set up while you are constructing the rest of the teapot. If you are planning to use a bamboo handle, pull two short lugs to attach to the pot.

Chapter opening art: Three porcelain teapots; Ruth McKinley, Canada, 1967. Paddled sides, white satin matt glaze, cone 10 reduction, wood-fired. *(Courtesy of the artist) (Photo by D. L. McKinley)*

LIDS

It's not that trimming lids is any more difficult than trimming anything else; the problem is in anchoring them so that you can get at them. For lids that aren't "flat" on top, like the knob style, or for other pots with narrow necks, a "chuck" is necessary to hold the form when turned upside down (Fig. 7–1).

The simplest form of chuck is a cylinder with a wide base and a flared-out rim. Chucks must be perfectly round and level at the rim. If you feel unsure about throwing your own forms for chucks, they can also be purchased from pottery supply houses.

To trim a pot with a narrow neck or a lid with a knob, invert it and set it on the chuck, anchoring it at the rim with soft pieces of clay if necessary. Then center the chuck on the wheel and attach it with soft wads of clay.

George has a third system which is much quicker but difficult for a beginner. He centers a wide, low "casserole-shaped" chuck full of sand. Then he pushes the pot to be trimmed, upside down, into the sand, which anchors the pot automatically (Fig. 7–2). It is hard for a beginner to get the pot to be trimmed both on center and level. But for production trimming, it really speeds up the process by eliminating the step of anchoring the pot and/or the chuck with wads of clay each time.

Stopper-Type Lids. The easiest way to trim a stopper-type lid is to anchor it, right-side-up, to the bat, pressing the three wads of clay down almost flat so they will go in under the rim and secure the short walls of the lid (Figs. 7–3 and 7–4). Use Surform to trim the curve of the lid and you probably won't need to do any other trimming.

Fig. 7-1 Anchoring bottle in chuck.

Fig. 7-2 Anchoring base of candleholder in sand.

Fig. 7-3 Anchoring a stopper-type lid to the bat.

Fig. 7-4 Anchoring a ginger jar lid.

Once you gain a little more control you may be able to trim a stopper lid right on its pot. This insures that you look at both together and trim a shape into the top that looks right with the bottom. This makes a *big* difference in the success or failure of this style lid.

Ginger Jar Lids. These should be treated as shallow bowls and centered and anchored upside down on the bat like a normal pot. Keep the wads of clay low so they don't interfere with the trimming tool. If you need to take off some of the height, turn the lid over and reanchor it, then use Surform on the rim until you have shaved it down enough. Sponge when you are done to smooth out the rim.

Flat Knob Lids. If thrown and measured properly, these should not need trimming. If they do need to be trimmed down a little, invert them in a chuck. (See preceding page on "chucks.") If you wet the rim of the chuck slightly, the lid may stick enough to stay there without anchoring it further. If

there is some sand in the chuck to weight it down, the sand may grab hold of the knob and anchor it automatically. If it does tend to wiggle around, take three small pieces of clay and put them on top of the rim of the chuck, then press your lid down onto them.

Recessed Lids. The easiest way to trim a recessed lid is upside down in its own pot (Fig. 7–5). A curve must be trimmed into the base, which should be measured again to make sure it fits through the flange opening. (See Fig. 7–6.)

Constructing the Teapot.
   1. Trim the body and lid to desired shape and weight. (See Fig. 7–7.)
   2. Cut the base of the spout at an angle —how sharp an angle will depend on the shape of your teapot base. Start with a shallow slant and keep increasing the angle (Figs. 7–8 and 7–9). Hold it up to the pot each time to check the shape. A good angle for a spout will (often) result in your being able to draw a straight line from the tip of the spout to the opposite bottom corner of

Fig. 7-5 Anchoring recessed lid upside down in pot.

Fig. 7-6 Different types of lids for same flange jar.

Fig. 7-7 The leather-hard covered jar, which will become a teapot.

Fig. 7-8 Holding the spout to the pot after it has been cut at an angle—to determine appropriateness, angle, and fit.

Fig. 7-9 Visual testing. Which of the two spouts do you prefer: the thrown tip in Fig. 7-8 or this carved-off tip?

71

Fig. 7-10 Scoring round base of spout to know where to drill strainer holes and where to cross-hatch pot before attaching spout.

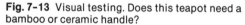

Fig. 7-11 Applying slip after strainer holes and cross-hatching are completed.

Fig. 7-12 Smoothing the bead of clay into both spout and pot to attach spout.

Fig. 7-13 Visual testing. Does this teapot need a bamboo or ceramic handle?

Fig. 7-14 A pulled handle.

the teapot. This enables you to pour all the liquid out of the pot. The spout should also be attached high enough so you can fill the pot to the top without any water coming out of the spout.

3. Draw a line on the teapot around the base of the spout where it is to be attached (Fig. 7-10). Set the spout aside and drill a few holes inside the circle you have just drawn. These holes will act as a strainer. Some people vary the size hole from bottom to top. Holes that are too small can clog up with glaze and fire shut later on. As a precaution, blow down the spout right after you have applied the liner glaze.

4. Cross-hatch over the line you drew—extending on both sides of it—and coat with slip (Fig. 7-11). Roll out a narrow coil of clay, long enough to go around the spout. Dip the base of the spout in water, and place it against the pot over the circle line. Holding it there with one hand, run the coil of clay around the base of the spout, smoothing it into the pot and the spout until the spout is smoothly joined to the pot (Fig. 7-12).

5. Attach the handle (see Lesson 4 on handles). Make sure it is directly *opposite* the spout and straight up and down. Check both visually and functionally for appropriate height and curve. (See Figs. 7-13 and 7-14.)

6. Drying. Since there are so many parts to the teapot, the safest way to dry it is to cover it with plastic for a day or two to equalize the moisture content. There is less risk of spouts or handles cracking off this way.

Fig. 7-15 Stoneware teapot; Bill Saks. *(Courtesy Jean Delius)*

Fig. 7-16 Stoneware tea set; Val Cushing. Spout construction left as decorative detail. *(Courtesy Jean Delius)*

Fig. 7-17 Porcelain liqueur set; Ruth McKinley, Canada, 1966. (Three bowls not shown.) Incised, filled and scraped decoration, cone 10-11 reduction, wood-fired. *(Courtesy Jean Delius)*

73

Three of our 40 students this year tried to make a teapot as well as a covered jar (see Fig. I-2, p. 5).

At the end of Lesson 7, we went on to the beginning of Lesson 8 and prepared earlier bisque-fired pots for glazing. It is easier if you can do this before actually applying the glaze, since it gives the wax a chance to dry.

Fig. 7-18 Porcelain teapot; Ruth McKinley, Canada, 1973. Cane bail handle, dipped slip, sprigged, ash-flashed, cone 10-11 reduction, wood-fired. *(Courtesy of the artist) (Photo by D. L. McKinley)*

Fig. 7-19 Dragon teapot; Pat Probst Gilman. Porcelain. *(Courtesy of the artist) (Photo by Ruth Pasquine)*

LESSON **8**

Glazing

Applying glaze to a bisqued pot is not a difficult process. However, practice and control are necessary for good results even in this area. The following instructions should help you develop a precise and direct method of glazing.

When our students arrive to glaze, we have all their pots bisque-fired and re-sorted back on their class wareboards. (In our studio, students sign their leather-hard pots and add a code number for their class so we can sort the pots more easily after they have all been mixed together for firing.) Besides the class wareboards, we also have a "lost and found" board—full of unidentifiable pots—and a "disaster" pile—pots whose bottoms blew out or cracked during bisque firing.

Also on hand at the beginning of the lesson are:

1. Buckets of glaze with cups for applying (see Section II on mixing your own glazes).

2. A small container of black stain (iron and cobalt oxides).

3. Bamboo brushes for applying stain or wax.

4. A container of wax. We use a wax emulsion that is available from ceramic supply catalogs and is usable at room temperature. The hazards of heated paraffin, which is extremely flammable, make it undesirable in a teaching situation —and even in a private studio. (Too many studio fires have been caused by forgotten paraffin on a hot plate.) If you do use paraffin on your own, use an electric frypan with a thermostatic control as a safety precaution.

BEFORE GLAZING

There are several ways to decorate bisque-fired pots before you apply glaze. And there are some things that should be done before you glaze the pots. These include sanding any rough spots on the bisqued pot and applying stain or wax. This is how we proceed with our small groups of students.

1. *Claiming.* Many students can't find one or two of their pots or are absolutely sure that the pots with their names on them aren't theirs at all. Between the shrinkage and the color change that have occurred as a result of bisque firing, the original pot has managed to "change" quite a bit. This, coupled with the tricks that memory and fantasy play, causes us to insist that everybody sign their work—even to those who say "Oh, I'll recognize it—who else would have make a pot like this?" All pots should be signed at some stage anyway. As a precaution against disappointment or hard feelings, we have students scratch in their names when the clay is soft, re-sign after trimming (in the bottom), and sign in stain before glazing. This may seem excessive, but it works.

2. *Sanding.* Even though we have paid careful attention at the leather-hard stage to trimming, smoothing handles in carefully, and sponging rough places etc., many pots need to have rough spots sanded before glaze is applied. Any kind of medium-grade sandpaper will do for this. Normally, in our own production schedule, we do this at bone dry, before bisque-firing; the clay smooths down more easily then. However, bone-dry pots are so fragile that we tend to keep the students away from them.

3. *Staining.* If you intend to sign the bottom of your pot with stain, sign *before* waxing. Stain will not cause the pot to stick to the shelf as will glaze, so it can be used on the bottom. The main purpose of our black stain is to sign all pots (again). But, it can also be used decoratively—under or over the glaze. The stain we use is strong, so we caution students to take it easy.

In the case of a handbuilt pot or a textured or stamped pot, stain can be sponged or brushed over the whole surface and then washed off with a clean damp sponge. Some stain will remain in the low spots and accent the recessed areas of the textured surface. (See Figs. 8-1 and 8-2.) This should be done on bisque-ware before glazing or instead of glazing.

Fig. 8-1 Decorative use of stain to highlight texture. Stain is applied heavily and washed off, leaving some in the indentations.

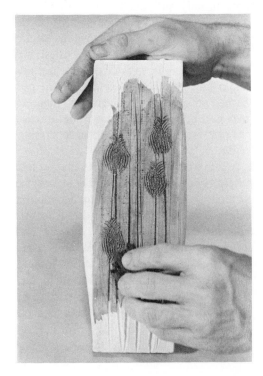

Fig. 8-2 Brushed-on stain for accent with glaze.

4. *Waxing.* Like staining, waxing is both functional and decorative. Wax is applied to those areas of a bisque-fired pot where no glaze is desired. During firing, pots usually sit directly on a kiln shelf. Therefore, no glaze can be present on the bottom of the pot, or it will cause the pot to fuse to the shelf. The easiest way to prevent this is to wax the bottom and about half an inch up the side of the pot. Some pots, such as hanging planters, may best be fired upside down; in this case, the *top rim* should be waxed or left free of glaze.

In a few cases, there are pots that we like covered *entirely* with glaze. These must be "stilted" on little three-pointed supports before firing. Normally, we don't do this with student pots, unless we have a bad feeling the glaze is on too thick and is going to run down onto the kiln shelf.

Covered jars must be waxed in two places. Not only do the bottoms need to be waxed so they can sit on the kiln shelf

without sticking, but the sections where lid and jar come in contact with each other must also be left free of glaze. See Fig. 8-3. The normal practice is to fire lids on top of jars to keep both from warping. This means that all glaze must be kept off both surfaces—rim of jar and edge of lid— wherever they touch. Otherwise you may end up with a closed form after they are fired.

The other use for wax is for decorating. If a design is painted on a bisqued pot with wax, no glaze will absorb into the pot along those lines, which, when fired, will be clay colored and will contrast with the glaze. It will be a clear sharp line if done right on the bisqueware. It will give a more muted line if you glaze the ware once *before* waxing the design, wax when the

Fig. 8-3 Functional waxing to prevent lids from sticking.

glaze is dry, and then reglaze in a contrasting color. We use wax-resist as a predominant method of decorating our own production ware; as a result our students tend to pick up on it.

Caution: Make sure the wax has dried —turned from white to clear in the case of the commercial wax-resist—before applying glaze. Both are water-base and will just mix together otherwise. The "resisting" quality of the wax works best once it's dry. Also be careful not to *drip* wax where you don't want it. It's very hard to get off and will need to be scraped or sanded.

Note: If these preliminary steps can be done in the class before glazing, it gives the wax plenty of time to dry. Then, in the next class, everybody can begin glazing right away. Applying glaze usually ends up taking more time than we expect.

GLAZING

What is the glaze? The first hurdle for some students is the awareness that glaze is not paint. It is not usually brushed on, it cannot be mixed together to form different colors (red and yellow don't make orange), and it looks entirely different in its raw state than it will after it's fired. The bucket of glaze that looks purple fires to a yellow-brown. (Beside each glaze bucket we usually leave a finished pot, labeled as to color, so the students can visualize the end result of their glazing.)

Basically, a glaze is clay in liquid form (in suspension) very similar to the engobes we were using at leather-hard. In addition, however, a glaze has a glass former (silica) added to give it the smooth surface, shiny or matt, and fluxes added that cause it to melt at a lower temperature. The color in the glaze comes from the addition of one or two oxides in very small amounts—iron, manganese, cobalt, copper, chrome, etc., are some of the more common coloring oxides. In reduction (a gas kiln), which is the way our students' pots will be fired, the oxides will behave somewhat differently than they would in oxidation (an electric kiln).

When and if you begin firing your own pots, you will probably be using an electric kiln. It is more convenient as well as being more predictable and easier to fire. (See Section II on electric kilns and electric kiln glazes). Certain decorating techniques may work better in the electric kiln, certain others in the gas kiln.

Besides depending on the atmosphere and final temperature of the kiln, the color and surface of the glaze also depends on the thickness of its application. Glazes need to be applied a little thicker for gas kiln firing, thinner for electric kiln firing. Some of the glaze color actually comes from the iron oxide in the clay body beneath the glaze in reduction firing. Speckles can also come from impurities in the clay body, which "bleed" through the glaze. If a colored engobe has been applied to the pot at leather hard, it will bleed through the glaze and change it too. The degree of color coming through from the clay beneath partly depends on how thickly the glaze coating is applied.

A glaze, especially when fired in reduction, does not produce one predictable reproducible color; it produces a range of colors—from blue to brown, for example, or from cream to rust. This range of color is affected by the temperature and atmosphere of the kiln, the color of the clay beneath the glaze, and the thickness of the glaze application, as well as the basic glaze recipe. (For more on gas kiln glazes and firing, see Section III.)

Decorating. At least one pot has already been decorated by using texture and/or engobe at the leather-hard stage. This should simply be dipped in a light semi-translucent glaze or left unglazed.

Usually the students try waxing designs on one or two of their pots as a second method of decorating. Some also stain designs on or sponge stain on decoratively before applying glaze.

A third option (besides the method of application—which can be used decoratively as well) is to brush on a shiny liner glaze in strokes or patterns. This will bleed through the matt glaze, cause it to break up, and make its color stronger—the matt blue-brown turns shiny bright blue, etc. This can also be done on top of the main glaze and is called *majolica*.

The method for applying glaze can also be used decoratively, since it will create thick and thin patterns. If a pot is dipped once down to a ridge, dried, and dipped again all the way down, the top section, which has been dipped twice, will be lighter in color. If a pot is dipped on one side, then on the other, and a third time to fill the spaces, a triangular pattern will evolve. Or a glaze can be poured irregularly over a pot, and runs and drips will develop in natural free patterns (Fig. 8-4).

Since *contamination* of glazes is a problem, we put one mug beside each bucket and encourage students to glaze a given pot with only one main glaze. We also tell them to be careful not to switch glaze mugs and to let their pots dry before redipping.

Fig. 8-4 Pouring glaze freely for irregular contrast in fired pot.

Applying Glaze. The normal way of applying glaze to your pot is to dip and pour. To glaze the inside, scoop some glaze out of the bucket with the glaze mug and pour it into your pot (Fig. 8-5). Turn your pot on edge and twist it around in a complete rotation, gradually pouring out the remaining glaze as you rotate (Fig. 8-6.) The entire inside should be evenly coated. Let this dry. To glaze the outside, hold the pot upside down and simply dip it, all the way down to your fingertips, into the glaze (Fig. 8-7), hold it there for five seconds or so, and remove it. The length of time you should hold the pot in the glaze depends on how thick the glaze is (approaching heavy cream, is about right for gas kiln glazes) and how porous a bisque your pots are (about 1000 °C works well for a bisque-firing temperature). Too thick a coating or

Fig. 8-5 Lining the inside of a pot with glaze.

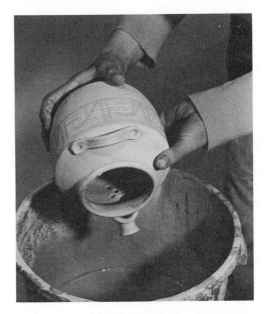

Fig. 8-6 Rotating the pot to coat entire surface.

too many coats may make the glaze "crawl."

Wipe the glaze off waxed surfaces. Even with the prior coating of wax on areas that were to remain unglazed, a certain amount of glaze will stick in little beads to the waxed surface. This should be sponged off.

Preventive Measures: In order to keep glaze from running all over the kiln shelves during firing (kiln shelves should be thoroughly coated with kilnwash before stacking), students should:

1. Feather the glaze back at the bottom edge so that it tapers down from its normal thickness to a very thin edge. This can be done with a sponge. Too thick an edge of glaze, even half an inch up from the bottom of a mug, for example, especially one with

Fig. 8-7 Kurt Wettlaufer demonstrating "most direct" method of applying glaze inside and out simultaneously.

Fig. 8-8 Whoops! A little too thick, or "thank goodness for kilnwash."

a curved side, will be very susceptible to running. (See Fig. 8-8.) The coating of wax which resisted the glaze originally, when you were applying it, is ineffective in preventing its running at high temperatures. In fact, by the time the glaze is molten, the wax has burned off completely.

2. Hold the pot by its bottom edge when dipping so the glaze runs back toward the top and away from that bottom edge. If you must hold it by the top rim because of an ungraspable bottom curve, turn it upside down as soon as you remove it from

the glaze bucket so the glaze will flow back toward the top as it dries.

Our glazes are matt and fairly stiff (except for the shiny liner we use for decorating). We ourselves almost never have to grind glaze and kilnwash off the bottom of production ware. But even with all these waxing and wiping precautions, a number of student pots will run and stick to the kilnwash of the shelves. This is a nuisance to us because the shelves will have to be recoated with kilnwash, and a nuisance to them because of all the grinding required (which we usually do for them because it's somewhat dangerous).

Reactions. Students coming back to claim their pots when we've finished firing them are usually amazed at the transformation. "They didn't come out at all like I expected" is the normal comment. The children never think the colors are bright enough. Our daughter repeatedly comments that she wishes we'd get some colors like the ones the school has (bright pastels, cone 04 electric). Most are excited and happy with the results, though, and ready to come back next year and try again.

CHAPTER 9

Continuing to Grow

When you first start throwing, you may be more interested in making things to use than in perfecting techniques and developing a certain style. Probably, with a little effort, you can bring both attitudes to the wheel with you. You are definitely going to want to do some experimenting to see what works best for you and what types of things you really want to do.

THROWING POTS IN SERIES

Throwing pots in series instead of one at a time, separates the intermediate potter from the beginner. Here are some types of series you may want to try.

Chapter opening art: Miniature tea set; George and Nancy Wettlaufer.

A Series of Mugs for the Purpose of Design and Control.

• Wedge up eight or ten half-pound balls of clay.

• Throw four mugs that are different shapes—experiment to make them visually pleasing as well as functionally acceptable. Try straight sides and curved sides, etc. Try tall, thin ones and short, squatty ones. What shapes and proportions do you like?

• Select the one that you like the best and make five more like it—as similar as you can without overworking the clay. Try to work quickly—three pulls, only five minutes per mug if possible.

You automatically have a *series for handles and trimming:* On the four mugs that are different shapes, try different styles of trimming, different sizes and shapes of handles attached at different

Fig. 9-1 Pair of stoneware bottles; Carl Sande.

Fig. 9-2 Large conical bowl and minature bud vase; Fung Chow. Blue-glazed stoneware. *(Courtesy Jean Delius)*

heights, etc. Think about how they look and how they will work; select the best style for your alike series of mugs and do those all the same.

What you have been doing is designing on the wheel—not in a notebook. It's the best way to come to a compromise between what you want to do and what the clay wants to do—and a much stronger, more spontaneous shape will emerge than if you had tried to throw from a preconceived sketch. (You also end up with some mugs for your personal use, so you haven't just been doing exercises.)

A Series for Curve and Flare Control.

• *For curve control,* try a series of vases —any size. Throw one almost straight up, coming to a narrow neck. Keeping the final neck size and the base size constant, try to make each succeeding vase more curved—they will be getting progressively shorter and progressively more bellied out (Fig. 9-1).

You can do the same thing with pitchers,

teapot bodies—even with closed forms, which are very good practice.

• *For flare control.* For beginners, we adopted a rule of thumb that they should try to keep the top of their pot more constricted (smaller diameter) than the base. Now it is time to start pulling up and *out* instead of always thinking up and in. Some of this may happen automatically, due to centrifugal force. The idea is to be able to control it. Try a "bread bowl" shape (see Fig. 9-2), and gradually flare it out wider and wider. See what the clay will and will not be able to do (use fairly stiff clay).

A Series for Rim and Foot Control. Throw a series of planter shapes that are all basically the same. Vary the rim in as many ways as you can think of, and vary the style of foot when you trim. You will be amazed at the different feeling a pot acquires by just these two modifications.

A Series for Size Control. Imagine that you are throwing an eight-piece canister set.

Fig. 9-3 George throwing a tall form.

Fig. 9-4 Stoneware vase; Val Cushing. *(Courtesy Jean Delius)*

Fig. 9-5 Stoneware vase; Bob Sperry. Bright cobalt brushwork. *(Courtesy Jean Delius)*

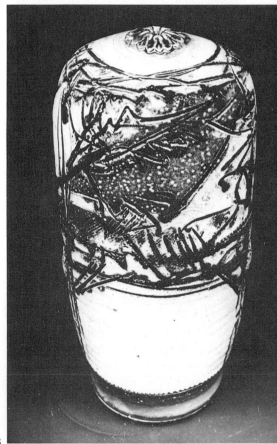

Fig. 9-6 Salt-glazed porcelain form; Regis C. Brodie. 16″ high. *(Courtesy of the artist) (Photo by Marcy Pesner)*

Fig. 9-7 Centering the top part of the hump.

Weigh out and wedge up balls of clay in half-pound increments. Start with two pounds. Make bases same size, and try to throw progressively taller cylinders (Figs. 9-3 to 9-6). The next time, try it in one-pound increments—you may not be able to control much over ten pounds on the wheel at first. Start with the smaller balls of clay and see how far you can get. You may also reach a point where the cylinder isn't getting any taller no matter how much clay you start with. When you seem to plateau, go back to working on smaller things, closed forms and miniature vases for example. See Figs. 9-7 through 9-10. Gradually the control will come.

Fig. 9-8 Opening the miniature pot.

Fig. 9-9 Using the tool inside to replace left hand, which no longer fits.

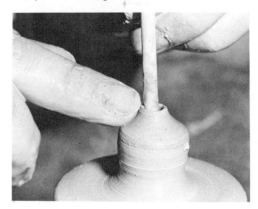

Fig. 9-10 Ready to cut off the hump.

Fig. 9-11 Centering clay for wide forms.

Fig. 9-12 Pulling out an even bottom.

Fig. 9-13 Flaring out the edge of a platter.

LEARNING TO THROW WIDER SHAPES

You must learn to center your clay very low and wide—this takes a lot of *down* pressure. As you form a plate, you must continue to press down while you are pulling the clay out to the side. (See Figs. 9-11, 9-12, and 9-13.) Even if you think you have thrown a good plate, your prob-lem may come later on in drying. Only part of the difficulty in making plates and platters is in throwing them. The other is in drying them without cracking—one side tends to dry faster than the other, causing unequal shrinkage and eventual cracking. Make sure to use *dry* bats if you do not string the plates. Turn leather-hard platters over so both sides can dry equally. Slow, even drying is important here.

Fig. 9-14 Stoneware platter; Steve Friedlander. Wax-resist design, two glazes. *(Courtesy Jim and Carol Reed)*

Fig. 9-15 Plate; Ishmael Soto, Mexico. White with bright blue owl glaze sgraffito. *(Courtesy Jean Delius)*

Fig. 9-16 Salad bowl; Alan Caiger-Smith, England. 13″ wide, deep blue-green with wax-resist brush decoration. (*Courtesy of the artist*)

Fig. 9-17 Stoneware bowl; Vivika and Otto Heino. *(Courtesy Jean Delius)*

Fig. 9-18 Hanging gro-lite planter; George and Nancy Wettlaufer. Two "bowls" trimmed with curved base to hang, holes and carving done at leather-hard stage, wax-resist glaze decoration.

EXERCISES FOR FUNCTIONAL CONTROL

Here's how to combat the "Well, I've thrown a cylinder, now what do I do with it?" syndrome. *Ask yourself* if you can carve it, put a lid on it, put a spout on it, put a handle on it, trim it to hang instead of sit, etc. Out of a wide-mouth cylinder with curved sides, we make our pitchers, hanging carved candleholders, sitting and hanging vases, and covered jars.

Out of a bowl shape, we make a hanging gro-lite planter, as shown in Fig. 9–18.

Out of a bottle shape, we make lamps and clocks (by paddling, carving, and adding handles), wine jugs, and plain bottles. (See Figs. 9–19 through 9–23.)

Out of closed forms, we make cheese shakers, piggy banks, butter dishes, egg-shaped planters, covered jars, teapots, and juicers. (See Figs. 9–24 through 9–32.) Closed forms are really adaptable, because once they have dried a little, they can be paddled into any shape, and an opening can be cut or carved out anywhere.

Fig. 9-19 Trimming and holes for lamp construction.

Fig. 9-20 Lamp fixtures.

Fig. 9-21 Finished lamp, from the authors' collection.

Fig. 9-22 Cut-out back of clock showing movement (formed from bottle paddled at leather hard and carved out).

Fig. 9-23 Front view of clock, from the authors' collection.

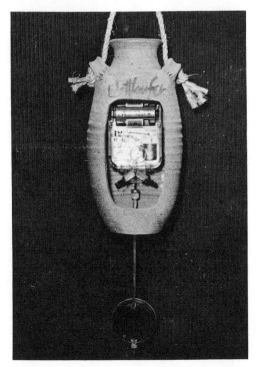

Fig. 9-24 Cutting hole for cork in closed-form cheese shaker (will have handle added shortly).

Fig. 9-25 Cheese shaker; George and Nancy Wettlaufer.

Fig. 9-26 Making a butter dish from a closed form; cutting apart closed form at base.

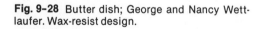

Fig. 9-27 Trimming plate half of butter dish.

Fig. 9-28 Butter dish; George and Nancy Wett-laufer. Wax-resist design.

Fig. 9-29 Cutting apart a closed form to make a covered jar; tool is held at an angle.

Fig. 9-30 Covered jar; Bill Alexander. Porcelain with gold luster. (*Courtesy Jean Delius*)

Fig. 9-31 Kerosene lantern; George and Nancy Wettlaufer.

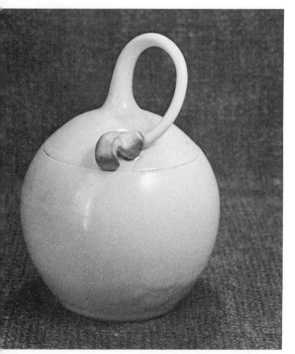

Fig. 9-32 Juicer; John Natale. Center thrown as closed form. (*Courtesy Jean Delius*)

EXERCISES FOR LEATHER-HARD DECORATING

Throw a series of planter shapes (or anything else), let them dry to leather hard, and trim them all the same. Go back to Lesson 3 on decorating, and try adding and subtracting clay in different ways alone and then in combination with engobes. Settle on one or two decorating techniques that have potential, and work them out further. Many potters stick with only one type of decorating and glazing for their whole production. This makes growth possible—slow growth, not hit or miss. Gradually, as you work on shapes and decorating ideas, you will discover that you have a "style" emerging. This will grow naturally and will come in conjunction with gaining control over the techniques of throwing as well as glazing and firing. Knowing your materials and what they can and can't do is as critical to the end result as is mastery over basic techniques.

CHAPTER **10**

Using the Pots You Make

When I (Nancy) first started making pots to keep, we "needed" hanging planters. (Everybody needs planters. They're still our best selling item today.) This turned out to be a good starting point, since almost any surface was acceptable—glazed or not, rough or smooth. All sorts of glaze defects that would have ruined mugs or bowls just added interest to the planters.

The first ones I made, though, were really too shallow. The water tended to run out the holes they were hung by. The ones I had put handles on (as much to practice pulling handles as for any other reason) worked better as far as depth went, but the handles tended to break if they were bumped (or mailed). So gradually I developed a type of planter I like to use— deep enough and wide enough that a clay pot will fit inside under the holes.

There's a running controversy over whether planters need drainage holes or not. We don't put drainage holes in our planters. Most of them hang in living rooms over rugs. To design an extra, saucer-type piece never really seemed necessary to us, although some people prefer them. We plant directly in pots without drainage and grow beautiful plants—a little gravel in the bottom is helpful. But we do make the pots big enough to accommodate a clay pot for those who want the extra drainage or who want to be able to switch plants from one pot to another.

(A bisque-fired planter substitutes very well for a commercial clay flowerpot—it's about the same porosity—so don't throw out your cracked bisque-ware; use it).

About the hangers: Don't make a nice pot and string it on a flimsy hanger. One problem is that natural materials like leather, hemp, jute, and manila will rot to varying degrees over a period of time. Macrame holders around the outside or handles on the outside of pots will help avoid this problem. Nylon or synthetic materials also avoid it, but somehow the artificial materials never look right with pots—although a really interesting effect can be had by hanging a large planter in the middle of a room on fifty-pound test fish line, which is practically invisible.

The second thing I decided we "needed" were some juice cups. This got me more into throwing in a series, which was good. The cups were o.k. (we're still using them), but the glaze surface wasn't all that great, and the bottom edges have chipped because I didn't trim them. Otherwise, they've stood up to everything except the lawn-

mower when the kids left them out in the grass. The same was true of the first mugs I made (we were pleased—the glaze was much better this time). In retrospect, the handles were really short. I hadn't quite mastered handles yet, and the mugs were kind of heavy once you filled them with coffee.

Then I overreacted and started throwing paper-thin cups and mugs that felt more like bone china than stoneware. They just sit on the shelf because they feel so fragile I don't enjoy using them. The mugs I like to drink out of best are about as wide as they are high—good for soup as well as tea or coffee. And they're very stable. Some

Fig. 10-1 Three stoneware hanging planters; Ruth McKinley, Canada, 1975. Carved decoration, ash-flashed, cone 9 reduction, wood-fired. *(Courtesy of the artist) (Photo by D. L. McKinley)*

people like shiny liners in their mugs so the tea or coffee doesn't stain, but we glaze the same inside as out.

Cups, mugs, and planters are reasonable things for beginners to throw successfully. They require perhaps the least technical skill and encourage one to throw in a series. However, a friend of mine who used to come over and work on the wheel with me decided that what she really needed was a set of plates, and she didn't think that throwing plates looked as hard as pulling up cylinders. This is not true at all, as she soon discovered. Most of them cracked in drying because of the unsure throwing and the uneven ridges in the bottom. So she abandoned that project.

One of the first things I bought from other potters (before we were making pots at all) were tall covered jars I could use as canisters, also tall pitchers—in fact, *anything tall*. After I started throwing myself, anything over six inches looked incredible —especially if it had, in addition, a well-fitting lid or a strong handle.

After living with these covered jars, I like some better than others—functionally. These might be some things to keep in mind if you are making your own or buying them from other potters. A couple are too narrow at the top to get a scoop into for flour or sugar, etc. One has a ginger jar style lid, which the large-handed potter that made it could undoubtedly grasp easily, but it tends to slip out of my small hands. A lid with a knob is really easier to handle. If it is the stopper-type lid, which has had a knob added to it, the rim of the jar tends to collect less flour and get less messy than it does in the case of a flange-type lid. See Fig. 10–2.

Casseroles with good lids that fit are also hard to get under control if you are making

Fig. 10–2 Adding knob to trimmed lid.

them yourself. For a long time, I made the wide lids of casseroles too thin and too flat and they tended to slump in firing. A domed lid works better on something wide. Finally George developed our style casserole, and we collaborate now. I make the handles and decorate it; he does the rest.

Stoneware by definition is ovenproof, if the body is formulated and fired correctly. Special clay bodies can also be bought or made that are flameproof; i.e., can be cooked with on burners as well as in the oven. However, do not assume that stoneware is more than ovenproof unless specifically stated.

Stoneware is also excellent for heat retention. A meal baked in a stoneware casserole will stay hot on the table for at least an hour. Once it cools, you can stick it in the freezer pot and all, then thaw it to room temperature, put it back in the oven, and then into the dishwasher. One of the reasons stoneware is so popular is because it is so functional.

Another thing the heat-retaining properties of stoneware make it great for is

Fig. 10-3 Scoring and adding slip for handles.

Fig. 10-4 Adding handles to casserole.

breadbowls. Large breadbowls are not for beginners to try, but once you've used one for making bread, you'll be inspired to work up to it.

Wine jugs and pitchers will stay cold for

several hours after being removed from the refrigerator. The same pitcher, if preheated with hot water, can be used to serve coffee, and retains heat just as well. A teapot will do the same. (See Lesson 7.)

Fig. 10-5 Soup tureen; George and Nancy Wettlaufer. Wax-resist design.

Fig. 10-6 Stoneware casserole; Carl Sande.

In general, most potters working in stoneware (cone 6 electric or cone 10 reduction) use lead-free glazes. Lead, although very useful as a flux at lower temperatures (cone 04), is not at all necessary at the higher temperatures. Even with a tag attached to all our pots saying they are lead-free, customers ask us constantly: "Are you sure it's all right to drink from this mug? . . . bake in this casserole?" etc. It is.

Once you begin appreciating what's involved in making good pots, you may end up buying more pots than you make. We still buy or barter nice pots—especially those in a style very unlike our own and especially from people we like—because we like to have them in our house. Pots are a kind of presence.

Fig. 10-7 Stoneware casserole; Val Cushing.

Fig. 10-8 Stoneware casserole; Michael and Harriet Cohen. Stamped decoration. *(Courtesy Jean Delius)*

Fig. 10-9 Stoneware casserole; Jack Masson. Pinched knobs for handles. *(Courtesy Jean Delius)*

Getting into Firing

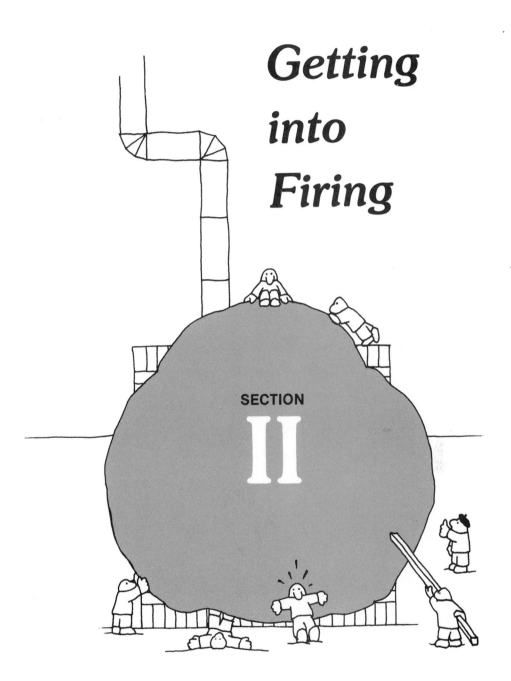

SECTION

II

CHAPTER **11**

Setting Up
a Studio

Pottery is becoming more and more feasible as a home hobby. Materials and equipment are now available in price ranges that an average family can afford. If you think of pottery as recreation for the whole family, an adequate set-up actually costs less than a sailboat, ski equipment for four, a snowmobile, or even a pool table. Once you know something about working with clay and glazes, and once you have a minimum amount of equipment, you can become self-sufficient.

We've been on both sides—learners getting into pottery with little formal instruction and teachers helping others get started. Our advice is based on our own experience.

We've found that many people think that they can just buy a wheel, some clay, and a few premixed glazes and they're all set to go. All they have to do is find a place to fire their pots. That's the problem. The marketplace is not yet set up for the intermediate hobby potter who has a wheel and is making pots but who has no kiln and needs a place to fire these pots.

In the pottery world, instruction, materials, and production are three separate businesses. Few people dealing in equipment and materials also give lessons or provide other services. They sell equipment. Instruction is available through schools and pottery studios, but usually neither of these sells supplies or fires work for the public. Production potters have their own set-ups. They make their own pots, fire them, and sell them. They usually won't fire pots for others. So the individual setting up a home studio is on his own to get it all together.

WHY WON'T POTTERS FIRE MY WORK?

If pottery were like photography and those who didn't have facilities could send their pots out to be developed, it might satisfy the needs of a hobby potter without a kiln —like a hobby photographer without a darkroom. But in pottery, it doesn't work that way. Pots are too fragile in the greenware or bisque stage to send out anywhere, and lots more work has to be done and decisions made.

Studio potters with firing facilities are often reluctant to fire work for others. The fact that a hobby potter is willing to pay for the service has little to do with it. Many potters are unwilling to take the risks and time to do it. Here are some of the reasons why.

Loss of Time Involved. Letting someone use your studio to glaze in (if they do not have their own glazes) causes interruptions in your working routine. Often you have to show people where things are, what to do, etc. Add to this the likelihood that you will have to spend time cleaning their brushes, putting things they've used away, and straightening up afterwards. Many studio potters feel it's just not worth it.

Danger of Glaze Contamination. In our studio, there are several buckets of glaze that look quite similar. Although they are labeled on the side, it has happened that a novice potter has mistakenly dipped a mug of glaze out of one bucket, poured it into his pot, and poured out the leftover glaze into the wrong glaze bucket. Oxide colorants are strong, so this kind of absent-mindedness can ruin a whole bucket of

glaze. It's a costly mistake and one that may not be detected until a whole kiln-full of pots has been fired. Several hundred dollars worth of production pots may have to be discarded if the contaminated glaze has been applied to production pieces.

The Danger of Kiln Accidents. Beginners who have not mastered the basic techniques of wedging and throwing or handbuilding may bring you work to fire that causes firing problems. Stacking or loading the kiln may be more difficult, since the pots may be oddly shaped. (Many production potters learn to "throw for a kiln." That means they know what to throw and how to fit it in.) You can lose valuable kiln space. This will increase the cost of fuel and may alter the gas flow patterns (in a gas kiln) enough to interfere with the whole firing process.

Even if the pieces happen to fit in the kiln conveniently, there are other potential dangers. Pots may explode or fall apart during firing because they were constructed improperly or had large air pockets in them. If this happens, any of the production ware that has pieces of flying pots stick to it is ruined. Molten glaze fuses the shards solidly onto the pots they land on. And if shards should land on the kiln shelf, it usually means hard work—stripping off old kiln wash and reapplying new to the shelf.

In addition, pots glazed by beginners may be glazed too thickly or have glaze too close to the bottom, so they stick to the shelf. In some cases, glaze has even run off beginner pots, along the shelf, and onto production ware on the shelf below.

There may also be problems in firing different clay bodies. Beginners are often unaware that the formulation of clay bodies differs according to the temperature they will be fired to eventually. It's not unusual for a beginner to use a low-fire talc body in art class. If the beginner then decides to use a production potter's high-fire glazes and kiln, firing problems may result. The low-fire clay body will actually melt into a glaze when fired to high temperatures. The beginner's pots will end up looking like cow flops, many of your pots may be ruined, and you may even lose some kiln shelves.

Misconceptions and False Expectations. Beginners who have never glazed or fired pots before don't understand firing problems. Often, the pots you fire for them don't turn out the way they envisioned them. You're likely to get the blame. The beginner will assume that something went wrong in the firing.

Occasionally, the opposite happens. The beginner pots come out beautifully. The glazes were good, the firing good, and the beginner is very pleased. Unfortunately, the beginner doesn't appreciate the fact that the success or failure of that pot was due to the knowledge and experience of the potter whose glazes he used and who fired the pots.

THE REWARDS OF DOING IT YOUR WAY

Even if you can find someone to fire your work, there are reasons why you should do it yourself. First of all, throwing or hand-building a pot is only the first step. The time spent on construction is minimal compared to the additional work that must be done to carry the pot through to completion. Glazing and firing can be as challenging and creative (and time-consuming) as working with clay. Actually, anyone can learn to throw a pot, with practice. Glazing and firing tend to be what separates the skilled potter from the novice. And you can't really call a pot your own if you are using someone else's glazes and kiln.

There are hobby ceramics studios that do sell glazes (at high prices) and fire pots to cone 04. But the glazes will come out shiny and will often contain lead, and the pots will often be too soft for functional use because they're fired at such a low temperature. In some larger cities, you might be able to find a place that fires pots to cone 10 reduction—traditional stoneware temperatures and atmosphere. Many even supply glazes that are less expensive and lead-free. This may be a good interim solution, but it's still best to have your own firing facilities—at least for the bisque firing so your pots don't break while you're transporting them.

Our advice to students, and others who ask, is to buy a small (2½ cubic foot) *electric* kiln that will fire to cone 6. It will probably cost around $200—but check with local hobby ceramics shops for a secondhand kiln first.

WHY FIRE ELECTRIC?

Many people think that the only way to get natural colors and matt glaze surfaces is to fire in a gas kiln. That's not true. Matt, stoneware-looking glazes are entirely possible in an electric kiln. (See p. 206 for our own cone 6 electric glaze formulas.)

People coming to our studio tell us that they've taken pottery courses at local museums or galleries where their pots were fired in an electric kiln and they came out awful. Then they take a course with us (we fire in a gas kiln), and they love their pots. They assume that if they ever get a kiln or build one, it should be gas. They equate good results with gas kiln firing. This is *not* necessarily so.

One reason our glazes are better is that we know more about our materials than a general art teacher without a ceramics background might know. We develop and mix our own glazes; often art teachers don't have or take the time to do it. If the art teacher had mixed his own glazes and added his own oxides, the results would probably have been much better—especially if the electric kiln went to cone 6.

The difference between firing to cone 04 (close to hobby ceramics temperatures) and to cone 6 electric (closer to stoneware temperatures) is significant. Cone 04 matt glazes are difficult but not impossible (see recipes on p. 205). If we were firing to cone 04, we would do much more with coloring the *clay* with oxides or adding engobes and do little or no glazing, except for liner glazes. Clay itself has the best matt surface going, a little rough for eating from, but otherwise beautiful alone—with *no glaze at all.*

For those who want to fire gas kilns before they have ever fired a pot, we say: It's something like setting up a darkroom to develop and print color photographs without ever having developed black and white first. Maybe you like color photography better than black and white. On the other hand, if you try it before you're ready, you might not end up with any photographs at all. Or maybe you'll get so discouraged you'll give up photography (or pottery) entirely.

What most people don't realize is that a *small* gas kiln is harder to control than a larger one. We still have to work at firing our gas kiln properly. A small one would be much worse. If you're new to firing, you shouldn't try controlling a gas kiln. Learn to mix your own glazes and fire *electric* first. You'll save yourself a lot of frustration.

Why We Recommend Electric. Here are some of the reasons we recommend electric kilns over gas for a beginner or a hobby potter:

• Results can be perfectly acceptable. Many potters fire electric by preference even when they have access to gas kilns.

• Electric kilns are within most zoning codes and can be used *inside* the house or apartment with little danger. In a pinch, small electric kilns can even be plugged into an electric range or dryer outlet. Gas kilns should be fired *outside,* partly because carbon monoxide fumes escape during reduction. And you'll probably need an extra structure for your gas kiln. Gas kilns are prohibited in many cities.

• Electric kilns are easier to fire. Except for turning switches up gradually, there's nothing to it. If your kiln has an automatic shut-off, you don't even need to be at home (but it's a good idea). Gas kilns present bigger firing problems. Heat flow and evenness of temperature must be controlled by the potter. And atmosphere is as important as temperature to the end result, another factor to worry about.

• Electric kiln firing is usually more appropriate for small quantities of ware. If you were to build a gas kiln, it would probably hold three times as much. So you would fire less frequently and not have the satisfaction of seeing your work completed. A smaller kiln allows you to fire more frequently, test glazes more often, and get some immediate feedback.

• Electric kiln firing is more consistent. And it's *cheaper*. You may be able to find a kiln secondhand. And you'll probably be firing at cone 6, instead of cone 10 (reduction). Firing to the slightly lower temperature will require less fuel. And your kiln furniture (shelves, posts, etc.) can be made of fire clay, which is much less expensive than the silicon carbide shelves required for firing to cone 10.

• Electric kilns are not wasted if you decide to build a fuel-burning kiln at a later date. An electric kiln, especially one with an automatic shut-off, is perfect for bisque firing. And if you move, you can take it with you. You won't have to take it apart brick-by-brick and put it back together again.

WHAT OUR STUDENTS HAVE DONE

Perhaps you're wondering what our students do as far as continuing with pottery after they've taken a course from us. Out of about 40 students each year:

• Five or six buy the type of wheel we use in class—the small, electric, variable-speed Spinning Tiger. Many live in apartments and don't have space for a whole studio and don't have a lot of spare time or money. This is really the only way they can continue with their throwing.

• One usually tries to build a wheel— from scratch or from a kit—with varying degrees of success.

• One may buy a more expensive wheel, either kick or electric, as a long-range investment with real hopes of eventually getting into pottery seriously.

• One or two buy (or already have from previous hobby ceramics classes) a small electric kiln—cone 6.

• One student may try to build a kiln. One student from past years is building one from a 55-gallon drum lined with fiberfrax.

• About half want to come back next year and take the course again. It's more feasible than getting their own studios set up. A few just take their pots and go home.

• Quite a few, maybe half, end up buying pots from us, realizing they won't be able to make anything comparable on their own for quite some time.

After six years of giving lessons, none of our "graduates" has really set up a complete studio and gone into competition with us selling pottery. One or two are finally getting pots out by bisque-firing their own and taking them to a place (about 100 miles away) to be glaze-fired.

This is not meant to discourage anyone. But you should be realistic about pottery as a home hobby. It's not like macrame or knitting. It's fairly complex, fairly expensive and relatively time-consuming. A lot of people are still prepared to try. And it's really rewarding once the initial investment in time and equipment is made.

WHAT EQUIPMENT YOU'LL NEED

If you're going to set up a studio, here are the minimum requirements:

1. *A Wheel*   at least $200
   [unless you build one (see following
   pages) or unless you are handbuilding]

2. *A Kiln* $250
   (for a small electric kiln, excluding
   furniture)

3. *Some Ready-Mixed Clay* $ 30
   (200 lbs @ 15¢ a lb)

4. *Tools* $ 10

5. *Clay and Glaze Materials* $100
   (see pp. 122–23)

6. *Miscellaneous* $100
   (scales, a 50-mesh screen, buckets,
   sponges, kiln furniture)

7. *Shelving Materials* $ 25
   (scrounge as much as possible)

8. *Books and Magazines* $ 25
                                               ─────
                                               $740

And once you have replenished the clay and glaze materials (reclaim your clay as much as possible), you're quickly up to $1000. This is not a lot of money for equipment. The only way to get into it for less is to scrounge a lot and build everything, but this takes time and a certain amount of know-how (also worth something) for adequate results.

Wheels. If you intend to buy a wheel, *do not buy something you haven't worked on.* If possible, try to find instruction somewhere so you know what throwing is all about. Try to use both basic types of wheel before you decide which to purchase. Basically there are kick wheels (with or without a motor) and electric wheels. Professional potters are pretty much split down the middle in preference. Some use one style, some the other. But in either case, a really professional wheel, one that will last a lifetime, will cost close to $500—new.

Try asking some potters what they recommend. Send away for some catalogs (check *Ceramics Monthly*). Read the article by Tom Lasher in *Studio Potter* (Winter '75) called "A Consumer's Guide to Wheels." Assess your own needs and resources: How much can you spend? Do you know enough to try to build your own? Are you transient or will you stay in one place for awhile? How much studio space will you have? Will children be working on your wheel?

Here are some of the reasons our students have bought the little Spinning Tiger electric wheels (there are also other brands on the market now in this price range):

1. It's what they learned on and all they know about. (Except for the Randall kick wheel, which costs close to $500. That's what *we* learned on, and we wouldn't use anything else.)

2. It costs under $200, and we did the ordering for them.

3. It's small, weighing only 20 pounds, so it's convenient and portable.

4. Some of the students had (or intend to have shortly) small children they wanted to involve in wheel work. Most kick wheels are too big for children, who can't stretch from the seat down to the flywheel. And the extra coordination of kicking makes it more difficult for them. (See the photos in Lesson 5 of our children working on the wheel. They've been at it since they were about 3—and they love it.)

On the other hand, if you are buying a wheel for a school classroom or as a lifetime investment, buy a more substantial wheel. Tom Lasher's article gives a professional wheel evaluation. He rates six different electric wheels and gives potters' comments about each one. The six rated are: Amaco (2–2a); Brent (CXC); Max (2000); Newton Potters (WGW–34); Oscar Paull (F 101); and Shimpo (RK–2). The price range (Winter '74–'75) is between $350 and $495. Good kick wheels are also available in the same price range.

The article also includes a fold-out sheet that lists distributors of kick wheels, kick wheel kits, motorized kick wheels, and electric wheels, with price lists and addresses.

Here are some of the things the professional potters interviewed talked about:

• *Criteria other than price* for evaluating a lifetime wheel: weight, noise, vibration, torque, and pedal drive. There were complaints that some variable-speed units in the pedals aren't sensitive enough for the speed range of electric wheels.

• *The plaster-bat-in-the-wheel-head* system for attaching and removing bats from the wheel. (Being able to remove bats is necessary for wider and larger pots.) One swears by each system, and one can't

stand each system. We have always used the plaster bat system with the Randall wheel and like it fine. But there is the danger of getting bits and pieces of plaster into your clay and creating real problems.

• *Horsepower ratings* on electric wheels. They're often misleading. It's a game played by manufacturers.

• *Schools on a tight budget* are recommended to buy one of each type wheel—electric and kick—to give students both types of experience.

Building a Wheel. If you are toying with the idea of *building a wheel,* ask yourself: Do you know what you're doing? Read some books; there are designs all over the place, and there are also kits available.

Fig. 11–2 Homemade poured-concrete wheel (frame welding done in a shop by a friend).

Fig. 11–1 Homemade wheel from a kit—plywood sandwich filled with bricks for flywheel.

(Charles Counts' book *Studio Potter* has a wheel design in it. Billie Luisi's book *Potworks* also has an extensive chapter on building your own wheel. Both are good books besides. Watson Guptill has a book out on building your own equipment. Check some of these first.)

One of the basic problems is balancing the flywheel to run true. This is necessary to be able to center the clay properly. It is doubly necessary if you are eventually planning to motorize the wheel.

Concrete poured into a tire tread makes a better flywheel than brick between plywood. (Some of the kit designs do the latter.) (See Figs. 11–1, 11–2, and 11–3.)

Incorporate a splash plan into the design. A problem with some of the homebuilt wheels we've seen (from a kit or from scratch) is the irritation of getting water from throwing all over the flywheel, making it slippery and impossible to drive with a motor. You also get water all over yourself. It's our opinion that splash pans aren't optional for beginners (even though some manufacturers don't include them with the basic wheel but sell them as an option).

It's hard to build your own wheel for under $75 by the time you finish buying bearings and parts (not including a motor). So unless you really enjoy tinkering with mechanical equipment, have access to a machine shop, or have no other alternative, our advice is to *buy* a wheel to begin with. Buy some premixed clay, some tools, and a small electric kiln and get on with potting. By the time you've finished building your own equipment, the whole desire to pot may have worn off. Or you may get so frustrated because your equipment is poorly built that your results won't be good enough to keep you inspired.

Fig. 11-3 Homemade motorized wheel.

Kilns. Buy a small electric kiln that fires to cone 6 until you've learned to fire properly. We've heard all your objections to electric kilns (and then some), but we still say that for the beginner and the hobby potter, it's the only reasonable way to go. When you know more about glazing and firing, or are into heavier volume, or have a larger or more permanent studio location, you may want to consider building a gas kiln. You may also want to stick with electric.

There are many electric kilns on the market. Electric kilns have been around for a long time because of the hobby ceramics market. Therefore, the easiest and probably closest place to check is the local hobby ceramics shop. Also check a publication called *Potluck Publications,* formerly *Ceramic Scope, Ceramic Hobby Industry Buyers Guide.* It costs only $4.00. (See the supplier list in the Appendix.)

Hobby ceramics shops are located everywhere. They are usually distributors for the major brands of electric kilns. (Be sure to specify high fire, though, because hobby ceramics people tend to fire to cone 04 or below.) Most kilns on the market now will go to cone 6. (For something higher, like porcelain, you are in a more specialized and more expensive range.) Hobby ceramics places may also know about secondhand kilns, although these are getting harder to come by. They will probably stock pyrometric cones at least for the lower temperatures and carry replacement elements for your kiln. They may even be able to get your kiln repaired for you or tell you who will do it.

Problems You May Have. If you can find a secondhand electric kiln, chances are it will need repairing. Here are some of the most common problems:

1. *Elements* burn out. If your elements have had glaze dropped on them or have gotten old, you may discover you cannot reach the proper temperature or it takes a long time to get there. You need a new element. Go to a hobby ceramics "authorized distributor" near you. They have an inventory of parts or will order them for you. They will need to know the model number of your kiln. Replacing an element is a matter of unscrewing two connections, removing the old element, and inserting the new one. Explicit instructions come with new elements. (Make sure the kiln is unplugged!) If some elements have "popped out" of their grooves during firing, they may need to be repositioned. To bend the elements, they must be *red hot.* Be sure to wear asbestos gloves!

2. *Firebrick* is very fragile and may need to be replaced often due to dropping the lid. Since insulating firebrick is very soft, it can easily be cut or grooved to size with a hacksaw blade. Use K–23 firebrick or its equivalent. If a brick is broken in the *side* of the kiln, just slide the replacement in. No mortar is necessary. In the *lid* or *door,* the easiest remedy is to patch the broken brick with kiln cement. Kiln cement is a mixture of fire clay and sodium silicate. You can buy it premixed, or mix your own. If you must replace a brick here, it will probably have to be cemented in place with kiln cement.

3. *Automatic shut-offs,* if damaged, can be purchased through a hobby ceramics dealer.

A kiln should last almost indefinitely if you take care of it and can perform these minor repairs.

Tools. You can sometimes get a starter tool kit. It should contain a needle tool, wood digger tool, cut-off string, elephant ear sponge, and perhaps a trimming tool. You will also need some bamboo brushes. At the beginning, this starter kit will give you the basics. Once you establish your preferences, you can order specific tools individually. You can also make your own tools. For example, a roll of 20-lb. test nylon fish line and some wood dowels will make a lifetime supply of cut-off strings.

The most important trimming tool, we feel, is a *Surform.* It is not generally available from ceramic suppliers. You can buy it from Sears or probably from large hardware stores. All you really need is the refill blade—it looks sort of like a long, flat cheese grater, and you can break it into two or three pieces for easier use. It was never intended as a pottery tool, but it certainly simplifies trimming. Our kids can even manage it.

Regular trimming tools come in many shapes. Try several different kinds. These become dull with age, and the metal edges can be filed or sharpened on a grinding wheel. An inexpensive grinding wheel is a good studio tool to purchase fairly soon. It is useful, both for sharpening tools and for grinding glaze off the bottoms of pots.

Fig. 11-4 Mixing clay in a cement mixer.

out clay scraps and abandoned pots. Slake them down, and skim off the excess water first. Then, add some ball clay while you are pugging the reclaimed clay to dry it out some more. Or, if your clay arrives a little too soft or too hard to work with, you will be able to run it through the pug mill, adding a little water or a little ball clay to adjust it.

A pug mill enables you to cycle and recycle your clay easily, preventing any waste. Economically, it makes a good deal of sense.

Production potters shy away from premixed clay because it may vary due to circumstances beyond their control. For example, a supplier may substitute one material for another without telling you, and your whole production may be affected. Problems like this are mainly for

Fig. 11-5 Running newly mixed clay through a pug mill.

Clay. It is interesting that many professional potters continue to buy clay ready-mixed, but always mix their own glazes. This is what we recommend for beginners as well. Why? Mixing clay is a hard job and can be done best with heavy equipment, which costs a lot of money. [At the moment, we mix our own clay in a cement mixer (Fig. 11-4). Then we put it through a pug mill (Fig. 11-5). This may be the cheapest way to go, and it costs about $1000 for a set-up.]

If you are teaching in a school, giving private lessons, or into a pretty high volume of clay, a *pug mill* is an extremely useful piece of equipment—more useful than a clay mixer. Even if you continue to buy your original clay ready-mixed, you will be able to repug the students' sloppy clay (or your own), mixing a little dry ball clay with it. Mush goes in one end and good throwing clay comes out the other end, ready for use. You can also reclaim dried

113

full-time production potters to sort out. If you are not a production potter, it's easiest to buy your clay ready-mixed. Use a pug mill to reclaim it.

Glazes. Although you can buy premixed clay, you should mix up your own glazes. To mix glazes, all you need is a gram scale and a screen ($50 to $75 worth of equipment as opposed to $1000 for mixing your own clay). The glazes will cost less than ready-mixed ones, and the end result will be much better. And mixing glazes isn't hard work. It's no harder than mixing up a cake in the kitchen.

Here are three things to keep in mind when buying glaze materials:

1. *Shortages* of certain materials are inevitable. We are living in a time of diminishing resources, and many raw materials are becoming scarce. This tends to boost their prices dramatically. (Tin oxide is a recent example of skyrocketing prices.) However, for the small quantity of coloring oxides the hobby potter uses, it's probably not really anything to worry about financially. If you feel strongly about it, you can eliminate all glaze recipes with tin oxide (or other scarce oxides) in them. But compared to the cost of buying premixed glazes of any kind, the money you save making your own makes the cost of oxides almost negligible.

2. *Toxicity* is a bigger problem. Everyone has heard of lead, which tends to be used frequently at low (cone 04 or lower) temperatures, because it is such a strong flux. Not only is lead very poisonous in its powdered forms, it is still potentially dangerous once it is fired. Lead will tend to leach out of functional ware filled with acids such as wine or orange juice. Any pottery glazed with lead is really unsafe to use with food.

For the home potter firing to cone 6 or above, lead is unnecessary. There are plenty of other fluxes. We recommend that the hobbyist stay away from all lead compounds—even if firing to cone 04. At low temperatures such as 04 or raku firing, substitute a *frit*. This is a glaze that has been fired, like glass, and ground up afterwards. It is a very good flux and glass former in low-fire glazes.

The teacher, or hobby potter with children, may also want to stay away from glazes that call for barium compounds for the same reason. They are normally used in matt glazes at higher temperatures. They are quite toxic *before* firing.

3. *Dust* is another health problem. Potters talk about silicosis as an occupational hazard. This is caused by inhaling clay dust, not in itself toxic but harmful if built up in the lungs. To guard against this, keep the dust down as much as possible in your studio, especially if it's in your house. Also get some 3-M-type face masks (available in supply catalogs), and wear them when you mix clay (if you mix your own), glazes, or when you clean the studio. Don't vacuum the studio. The clay particles are so fine they go right through the vacuum cleaner bags, clog up filters and motors, and cause general distress. Wear a mask and sweep or hose down the floors. Then get out for a while.

If you are firing in your home, you will also want a fan. Sulphur tends to burn off many clays during firing, and the fumes are quite acrid. A school art room should also be ventilated in some way. If your studio has a window, install a fan in it, and suck the fumes out that way. A hood, like those for electric ranges, will also work well, but it costs more.

FURTHER INSTRUCTION

If you are interested in learning more than what you can accomplish on your own, there are lists of available instruction. One such list comes from the American Crafts Council. A very useful book for this is a paperback called *By Hand.* Hobby potters as well as school guidance personnel will find this book very informative. It is divided up by state and lists schools and studios that instruct crafts (not just pottery). There are also places that give two-week concentrations or intensive courses, especially during the summer. They're on a first come, first served basis. No credit or entrance requirements. (Book early for these; they're in big demand.) And there are some craft-instruction-for-the-whole-family types of summer camps. See the Bibliography for more details.

To keep yourself informed, both as a consumer and a learner, your best bet is to begin subscribing to *Ceramics Monthly.* It lists summer instructional sessions and workshops, craft fairs and exhibits, audio-visual aids for teachers, etc. Many articles are worthwhile, even for beginners. Pictures may inspire you, and the ads from suppliers are useful. Send away for catalogs if you're a potential customer.

Studio Potter is an excellent publication but is probably more useful to the professional or more experienced potter. It carries no ads for equipment or supplies, so it's less useful from a consumer standpoint.

However, some articles evaluating equipment or giving directions for building equipment have been extremely useful, even for a beginner.

There is no way we can do an exhaustive survey of suppliers. (We've done a small one; see Appendix A.) But in the hopes that it may be helpful, we are listing the various suppliers we deal with. It should give you an idea of where to begin.

Locally (we live west of Syracuse, New York, in the Finger Lakes Region), we buy propane from a local LP Gas dealer (Bobbett Gas). We buy refills for our gas analyzer (for reduction firing) from Syracuse Oil Burner Supply. We buy burners and jute in 50-lb. rolls from an industrial supply place, Delo Corporation, in Syracuse. We buy a lot of hardware and plumbing supplies locally. We buy firebrick plus kaowool for stuffing the cracks of the kiln, from R.J. Denton, a refractories company in Syracuse. We buy a lot of clay and glaze materials, plus tools and odds and ends, from Miller Ceramics in nearby Weedsport, who carries most pottery supplies including wheels and kilns, silicon carbide slabs, etc. We buy heavy materials there to save shipping costs.

We order a number of things by mail through catalogs. *Minnesota Clay Company* is one such general supplier. They carry 3–M masks, wax-resist, raku tongs, books, bamboo handles, etc. We get our corks from Phoenix Design in Chicago. For nonclay accessories other than corks, we order in bulk from wholesalers. (Wholesalers usually have minimum order requirements that are too high for the average hobby potter.) We get leather for hanging planters from *Caldwell Lace and Leather* in Auburn, Kentucky. They offer a discount on 500 or more laces. Clock movements come from Empire Clock, 1295 Rice Street, St. Paul, Minnesota. Lamp parts come from Angelo Brothers in Philadelphia (a large-volume wholesaler). For small quantities of everything, deal locally or check *Potluck Publications,* formerly *Ceramic Scope* magazine (listed in Appendix A).

You'll have to spend some time ordering materials and supplies. And you'll have to deal with a number of places. Once you find out what you can get and where to get it, half your work is done.

CHAPTER 12

Firing—
A Simple
Progression

As we've said before, firing in an electric kiln is the easiest and best way for a beginner to get into firing. We're going to try to get you started firing with a simple step-by-step progression. You'll learn to handle the kiln and glazes and to work within their limits. If you master the basics and apply a little imagination, you'll get excellent results. We'll point out trouble spots and special techniques along the way.

Many people complain that firing in an electric kiln gives them ugly, shiny glazes. They think that it's the kiln's fault and if they use a fuel-burning kiln they'll get fantastic results. Not so. Usually the basic problem with electric kiln firing is not the kiln, it's the glazes. Switching to a gas kiln won't solve your problems. Try mixing your own glazes—you'll probably be much better off.

But, *remember:* You don't *always* have to glaze your pots. The idea isn't to make a pot and then cover it up with glaze. Keep in mind that glaze isn't your only source of color. In fact, it is best for you to think of glaze primarily as a *surface*—smooth as opposed to the rougher surface of the clay. Glaze may not always be necessary—except to prevent seepage. In that case, use a clear liner. And color isn't your only (or even primary) means of decorating. Don't assume that you construct first and decorate second, that you construct with clay and decorate with glaze.

DECORATING WITHOUT GLAZES

Working Directly With the Clay for Color. If you know nothing about glazing and are afraid to try it, try this: Instead of adding oxides to a base glaze for color, try adding oxides to your clay body. A light clay body works best for this. Mix the oxides into the clay in slip form. If you buy your clay ready-mixed, slice chunks of it into narrow strips, powder them with oxide, then wedge them *thoroughly* back together. If the idea appeals to you, get a copy of Berensohn's book *Finding One's Way With Clay.*

For the proportions of clay to oxide: Start with 5–10% of an oxide. Use cobalt (blue); chrome or copper (green); manganese (brown); or vanadium stain (yellow) to begin with.

If you are handbuilding, you can use different-colored clays in the actual construction. If you are working with slabs or on the wheel, it may be easier to add contrasting color by means of a brush or by-dipping leather-hard pots into colored engobes. Both colored engobes and colored clay are basically the same, except that one is in slip form and the other is plastic clay.

This is a very direct and extremely effective way of working with clay. You do your decorating at the *same time* as your constructing. You'll know how your pot will look as soon as you've finished constructing it. No need to keep one idea in mind while you're making the pot, then wait until it dries and is bisque fired, and then start glazing—all the while hoping that you remember what you had in mind in the beginning. (See Fig. 12–1.) Students and beginners who have trouble visualizing the end result of their work may find this the best way to work. It's immediate and satisfying.

Working with different colors in the clay gives you other options, too. Since you're working at the leather-hard or softer stage, you can still add texture to your pot. It is also one of the few techniques that is equally effective at any temperature.

Staining. If you are using colored clays and engobes and intend to leave the piece unglazed, or if you have incorporated

Fig. 12–1 Test for clay color.

texture or relief into the surface for decorating, you may want to accentuate these effects. Try staining your pot after it has been bisque-fired. Brush stain into the recessed areas, and then wipe all the rest off. (See Carlton Ball's *Pottery Making Without a Wheel,* for texturing and staining ideas.)

If you feel you don't really understand glazes yet, or have had some bad experiences with ugly, shiny commercial glazes, approach the problem this way: Omit glazing. Work with colored clay and engobe for color contrasts, texture for surface interest, and stain for accents. At the most, all you'll need is a clear glaze on the inside to keep the pot from leaking.

Work With White Glaze. If you prefer not to use colored clays and engobes for your color, or don't want *any* color, or would like to get on with the business of glazes, there are four simple approaches. They are all based on the use of a white glaze that you can make up from a clear commercial glaze you've bought. The easiest way is to add *zircopax* to it. This is a good material to have on hand, so buy ten pounds of it as a starter. Add about 20% (by weight) to your clear glaze. This will *opacify* the glaze—make it white instead of transparent and slightly more matt. If you prefer a very matt surface, try adding a little ball clay. (You should have ball clay on hand for reclaiming clay anyway.)

If you already have a stockpile of shiny commercial glazes and want to make them more matt, try adding clay in graduated proportions. Start with half, and go up or down from there. Again, you are adjusting the *surface,* the most important quality of your glaze. Here are some effects you can try.

All White—No Color at All. Look at the pictures of Pat Probst Gilman's work (see Figs. 7–19 and 12–22). You may want to try an all-white effect. Hers is white porcelain with a clear glaze. It's fired to cone 12. You'll probably want to stick with cone 6, but you can approach this effect. Use a very light or white clay body, add interest by texturing, incising, modeling, etc. Then glaze with your white glaze. This is not to suggest that you should copy her style, only that working in the absence of color is very effective and might be something you'd like to try.

Contrasting with White. Use your white glaze over a dark (red, brown, or black) clay body, leaving sections of the darker clay exposed. Dansk dishes, made commercially, work on this design principle.

White inside and dark clay outside give both a light-dark value contrast and a rough-smooth surface texture contrast. This procedure can also be used very effectively with wax-resist patterns, permitting the dark clay body to show in designs that contrast strongly with the white glaze. Blackbird Clay (or Barnard), alone or mixed with water to slip consistency, makes a good chocolate brown engobe at cone 6 and a black matt glaze at cone 9 (oxidation).

Rubber-Stamping an Oxide Over a White Glaze. Glaze a pot with a plain white glaze as described earlier and let it dry. Mix a small amount of Wesson oil with an oxide —cobalt oxide works well for a blue, iron oxide for a black, etc. Take something like a tongue depressor and spread a thin layer of this oil-oxide mixture on a piece of paper towel—an easy kind of homemade stamp pad. Make a rubber stamp by cutting your own shape out of a thin sheet of sponge rubber and gluing it onto a block of wood. Or use commercial sponge-rubber shapes. (A children's set is made by Childcraft.)

Just press the rubber stamp into the

Fig. 12-2 Rubber-stamping a pot.

oxide mixture on the paper towel. Check to make sure that you have an even coating on the sponge. Then press it onto the glazed pot in a border or random design. (See Fig. 12–2.) This should be done over the glaze, because the oil acts as a resist (like wax), and if used under the glaze, it will inhibit it from covering the stamped areas. Rubber-stamping is an easy and effective way of decorating, and it's especially fun for kids.

Dissolve Coloring Oxides. The same oxides you used for coloring clay and engobes can be dissolved in water. (Try them one at a time.) Mix two or three tablespoons with a pint of water, weaker in the case of cobalt or chrome. Apply your white glaze, and let it dry. Then with a brush dipped in one of the dissolved oxides, brush strokes or paint designs on your pot. Think of your white pot as a blank canvas to paint on.

As a variation, try dipping your pot in white glaze and letting it dry, painting a design on with wax, then brushing or sponging the dissolved oxide over the whole pot. After firing, this will look as if you used a colored glaze. It is actually the next best thing to adding oxides to the glaze directly. It will give you a good sense of how little coloring oxide is necessary and, proportionally, how much of a glaze is actually the "base" or plain surface.

We discovered this year that this technique also works very well with raku firing. We had pinched some pots with different-colored clays, so we wanted a clear glaze for those. We mixed up one bucket of clear base for everybody, and then had on hand small containers of various coloring oxides diluted in water. That way those who wanted to could brush them on their glazed pots, either over the whole surface to look like a colored glaze or in strokes and patterns for a contrasting design. It made glazing much easier. We didn't have to mix up eight or ten different glaze batches. And it gave us more decorating flexibility.

You may now want to try the next step— mixing the oxides directly into your base. If you don't have a gram scale, try using three teaspoons of oxide per pound of dry glaze for all but cobalt and chrome. Use less than one teaspoon for those.

White Glaze Plus Albany Slip. Another effective and simple thing you can do (still without mixing a glaze from scratch) is to buy some Albany Slip to use in combination with your white. Albany Slip is a natural glaze that comes out of the ground ready to use. (The shiny brown insulators on telephone poles and electrical wires were glazed in Albany Slip.) Buy 10 lbs. of it from a supplier and mix a small amount with water to glaze consistency. This can be applied either over or under your white glaze. It will result in a nice mottled effect. With these two glazes, applied separately or in different combinations, you will have quite a wide range of different effects. Dip them geometrically. Pour them freely. Wax resist one over the other, etc., etc. If you are going to pursue this mottled effect, this may be the time to think about adding some specks to your clay body. Granular illmenite works well. Just wedge some in *before* throwing. These will bleed through from the body to the glaze and give it a nice speckled surface.

Photographic Silkscreening. If you know something about photography, this white base glaze is a good surface for photographic silkscreening. You can either do it directly on the pot or with prescreened decals. We have become interested enough in this process ourselves to be thinking in terms of returning to electric kiln firing for some of our work.

So Here You Are. You've been able to do a great deal and learn most of the basics involved in mixing and firing your own glazes. All this *without* using those "awful, shiny commercial glazes" that you knew you'd hate and without buying a costly gram scale or mixing up a glaze from scratch. You know what an opacifier does to a transparent glaze. You know how to change the surface of any glaze from shiny to matt. You know about oxides diluted in water for color or decoration over or under your white glaze. And you've learned how to get a broken up mottled surface by using white and Albany Slip in combination. That will keep you busy and give you a lot of variety for quite a while—especially if you are still trying out the possibilities of using colored clays and engobes and different textures for decorating.

And, surprisingly enough, you haven't spent a lot of money:

GLAZE MATERIALS SHOPPING LIST SO FAR

Some light clay body in powder form for adding oxides for engobe treatment....................	$ 5–10
Some ball clay to put back into your clay for reclaiming and to use as a glaze-matting agent	$ 5
One clear glaze, powder or ready-mixed (about $1.00 per lb.)............	$10
Some Albany Slip glaze (10 lbs.)	$ 5
Some Zircopax (five or ten lbs.).......	$ 3–6
Some coloring oxides (cobalt for blue; chrome, copper for green; vanadium stain for yellow; rutile for buff-orange; iron for brown)	$20

Note: *If you haven't bought a screen for mixing up glazes, you can use an old nylon stocking temporarily. An old blender works well, too, but clay materials are very abrasive and wear out machinery quickly. If you intend to continue, a screen and a gram scale are necessary.*

MIXING GLAZES FROM SCRATCH

Until recently, the hobby pottery market has not been great enough for suppliers to worry about selling good quality cone 6 electric kiln glazes. But interesting glazes are now becoming available due to the tremendous surge of interest in pottery both as a home hobby and as school and college courses. As an experiment, it would be worth ordering a few ready-mixed glazes from suppliers and trying them, alone and in combinations.

You'll still have problems, though, not the least of which will be the expense. We suggest that you take the following shopping list, buy yourself a gram scale and a few more raw materials, and mix up your own glazes. It will end up saving you money, and your results will probably be better.

In addition, buying glazes without understanding their components is never a good idea. It's like buying an "A" string without knowing how to tune a violin. Knowing the essential characteristics of the glaze materials will help you to know how to make adjustments if things go wrong. For example, if you want a more matt surface, you can add more clay. If you want it shinier, you can add a flux or silica. If a color is too strong or too weak, you can adjust the oxide concentration. If your glaze is crazing or crawling, you can make appropriate adjustments in formula or application.

So that even if good glazes become available commercially at reasonable prices, there is a certain amount of fine tuning that you must always do yourself. Accept the challenge of mixing up some glazes from scratch, getting an acceptable base glaze, and experimenting with oxide additions for color. Spend some time learning about your materials. That's what craftsmanship is all about. Too many decisions are made in the glazing and firing half of your work for you to give up control after you've finished constructing your pot. The satisfaction of breaking through the mysterious fog of glazing and firing will be great enough to be worth the time and effort involved.

Budgeting Your Time. To this day, we spend only about 10% of our time on the wheel making our pots. When you are making pots for fun or just learning, throwing may seem like the most important and time-consuming part of pottery. Trimming may seem a nuisance. Stacking and bisque-firing seem just odd jobs, mixing up glazes and applying them another menial chore, not to mention buying supplies, cleaning the studio, reclaiming clay, etc. But each of these activities is important. And if you plan, from the beginning, to spend time and give attention to these "details," you'll be less impatient. And plan to spend some time experimenting with and adjusting glazes. It takes time, but it's the only way you'll get in touch with the materials you're creating with.

SHOPPING LIST FOR GLAZING FROM SCRATCH

Gram scale and screen	$ 50
100 lbs. feldspar (we use C–6 soda spar)	$ 10
25 lbs. zinc oxide (ZnO)	$ 20
50 lbs. whiting (CaCO₃)	$ 5
50 lbs. ball clay	$ 3
50 lbs. flint (silica, SiO₂)	$ 4

Note: *This may seem like a greater quantity than you'll need. But you'll pay almost as much for any smaller quantity. Some bags may be labeled with a manufacturer's name instead of the name of the material. For example, "Atomite" is a brand name for whiting. Label your bags clearly with the material name, especially in the classroom. You'll need to know what you have.*

For experimenting, buy small quantities of the following:

5 lbs. wollastonite	$ 2
5 lbs. talc	$ 2
5 lbs. dolomite	$ 2

Also Albany Slip, Barnard, or Blackbird clay listed earlier, and coloring oxides, if you have not already purchased these. If you have a little extra money, you might want to buy a drill extension. This is a beater on a long shaft that fits into a power drill. It's very useful for mixing up glazes. It costs around $5–$7.

A Good Basic Glaze Recipe. If you like matt glazes, here's a recipe for a four-component glaze that we used when we began firing electric and wanted to get a stoneware look. We've given it to lots of friends, both hobby potters and art teachers firing to cone 6 electric, and all have been pleased.

C–6 MATT GLAZE (CONE 6 OXIDATION)

	%	1000-gram batch
C–6 Spar (a soda spar)	45	450g
Whiting (CaCO₃)	18	180g
Ball clay	25	250g
Zinc oxide	12	120g
Water 1200g		

Note: *45% means 45 grams in a 100-gram batch or 450 grams in a 1000-gram batch. 450 grams equal approximately one pound.*

Try the following oxides with it:

Rutile	2-5% for a light tan to gray
Manganese dioxide	3-5% for a brown
Copper oxide	1-5% for green to almost black
Iron oxide	3% for tan to mustard
Cobalt oxide	¼-½% for light to dark blue

Keep some of the base glaze plain, and use it in combination with the colored glazes. One over the other produces a nice broken-up surface.

Adjustments: To get the same surface at cone 2, add 12% silica or 8% colemanite. (Silica adds more glass former, colemanite more flux. The end result is similar.) When fired at cone 9, C-6 glaze makes a nice white liner glaze. To get a more matt surface at cone 9, add 15% alumina, 10% more clay, and reduce the zinc oxide. For a softer surface at cone 6, add 8–10% colemanite.

Firing Time: In a small electric kiln, fire 8 to 10 hours up to temperature. Normally, the kiln cools at its own rate, but the cooling rate can affect the surface.

Mixing. Weigh out the dry ingredients with your gram scale (Figs. 12–3 and 12–4). Set them aside in a small plastic container or

Fig. 12-3 Weighing out base glaze materials.

anything suitable. (In these recipes, 1% equals 1 gram.)

Then weigh out the water, an equal amount by weight or a little more. About 55% of the total mixed batch is water; the other 45% is glaze materials. Put most of the water into a container. For a small batch of glaze, you can use a 2- or 3-lb. coffee can.

Add the dry ingredients to the water, stirring briskly with a wire wisk or the drill mixer (Fig. 12–5). Gradually add the rest of the water, as you need it. Your mixed glaze should be a little thinner than heavy cream.

Screen Your Glaze. Get another container. Put the screen on top of it and pour your glaze through the screen (Fig. 12–6), stirring with your fingers to break up lumps. Discard any foreign matter remaining on top of the screen. Rescreen back into the original container.

In time, clay settles out and the glaze needs to be remixed and rescreened before using. One way of reducing this tendency is to add 1–2% of bentonite. This helps to keep the glaze materials in suspension. Another method is to use about ¼ teaspoon of epsom salts per gallon of glaze as a starter. Mix the epsom salts in a small amount of warm water before adding it to the glaze. How much you'll need depends on many things, but most important is the amount and kind of clay materials in the base glaze. A second ¼ teaspoon can be added, but be careful as it could cause the glaze to gel. What you're doing with the epsom salts is called "flocculating" the glaze.

You'll discover that equal volumes do not weigh the same amount when you're weighing out glaze components. This is because they all have different densities. Formulas for glazes are almost always written in weights. That's why you need a gram scale. Volume measurements aren't accurate enough. To give you a rough idea of the corresponding volumes of material in cups and spoons, we have rewritten the recipe for a 1000-gram batch. It's not completely accurate, since the volume also depends on the particle size of the materials and how packed down they are.

C–6 GLAZE—
REWRITTEN BY APPROXIMATE VOLUME

C–6 spar	2¼ cups	(450 g)
Whiting	⅞ cup	(175 g)
Ball clay	2 cups	(250 g)
Zinc oxide.	⅓ cup	(125 g)

(For oxide additions, 1 teaspoon per lb, 2 teaspoons/1000-g batch (dry) equals about 1%.)

You can make other observations about your glaze batch. It doesn't look like paint.

Fig. 12-4 Weighing out oxide additions.

Fig. 12-6 Screening.

Fig. 12-5 Mixing up the glaze.

Fig. 12-7 Glaze tests ready for firing.

It probably doesn't look anything like the color it will fire to. Unless you are using frits, which are more like stains and have been pre-reacted, a raw glaze batch is a much different color than the fired glaze. See Fig. 12–7.

If you feel the dry materials as you mix up your batch, you can tell that this is basically clay in slip form. All the materials found in this glaze recipe (except the zinc oxide, which is a flux) are present in clay bodies but in different proportions. The glaze and the clay body are two similar materials. The difference is that one, the glaze, has more flux in it so that it will begin to fuse. The other, the clay, retains its shape, fusing only enough to become dense (nonporous) but not enough to slump or flow the way a glaze does.

On cooling, both clay and glaze must shrink equally so that the glaze, which has fused into and become part of the surface of the clay, is not stressed to such a degree that it begins to craze or crackle. This is a common problem, since the additional fluxes in a glaze cause it to shrink slightly more than the clay body. Glazing pots is not like baking a cake, which you can decorate and cover up later. These problems are due more to the relationship between the glaze and the clay as they are fired together than to one or the other alone.

Simply, a glaze is a clay to which a flux has been added. Actually a cone 04 clay body will *become* a glaze when fired to cone 9. In slightly different terms, a glaze is a glass (silica), to which a flux (soda or potash) has been added to make it melt at a lower temperature than it normally would ($1713\,°C$), and a hardener (alumina) to make it more viscous (keep it from flowing off the pot).

In the glaze recipe we have just given you, the silica is present in the clay ($Al_2O_3 \cdot 2SiO_2 \cdot 2H_2O$) and in the feldspar. Feldspar, which has one flux (soda, in this case Na) and six alumina to one silica molecule, is a clay material. It hasn't suffered the leaching action of weather and, as a result, retains a certain amount of flux (soda or potash) in addition to the alumina and silica that are present in clays. The alumina, required to keep the glaze from flowing off the pot, is present both in the clay and the feldspar in the glaze recipe. Since the feldspar itself does not have enough fluxing effect for this glaze to mature at cone 6, other fluxes are added. In this case, they are whiting (calcium carbonate) and zinc oxide, which are added in small amounts. Talc or colemanite could also be used as fluxes with very little difference.

The base glaze, a clay in suspension with a flux and a glass former added, can take on colorants in the form of oxides. The reaction of the coloring oxides is affected by the composition of the base glaze in two ways. A shiny glaze will give a stronger color than a matt glaze with the same amount of oxide added. And certain materials in a base will affect the oxide colorants. Cobalt, which normally produces blue, will produce lavender in a magnesia-based glaze (one containing dolomite or talc). In addition, some color will come through from the coloring agents in the clay body to which the glaze has been applied. This is especially true of iron oxide, which burns through from the reddish-colored body to the glaze. It's also true of granular illmenite or other speckles.

Variations on a Theme. You don't need a lot of different glaze recipes. We have talked about varying the oxides and their percentages for color changes and of varying the clay and silica ratio for shiny-matt surface changes. Actually, all the materials of a glaze can be varied and substituted for different effects. One, or at most two, base glazes that work well are all you'll need. Even as production potters, we basically use one matt glaze recipe with variations and a shiny liner.

Here's a matrix of adjustments for different materials beginning with the C-6 recipe as the base:

	C–6	X–S	SH	C6W	18
C–6 spar (soda)	45	40	50	33	40
Whiting	18	20	10		15
Ball Clay	25	10	20	25	20
Zinc oxide	12	5	10	12	
Silica (flint)		20			15
Zircopax		20			
Talc			15		
Wollastonite				30	
Dolomite					10

XS is a glaze with a shiny surface. Look at the change in materials. Much of the clay was taken out and replaced with silica, the glass former. The zircopax was added to opacify it for a white liner. Without it, it would be clear.

SH is also shiny but not as shiny as XS. The addition of talc to the C–6 glaze, a flux at this temperature, and the deletion of some clay, indicate that this will be shinier than C–6.

C6W has added wollastonite, a calcium silicate (whiting is a calcium carbonate). It's a natural material containing both calcium and silica and works well in glazes at this temperature. C6W has a matt surface like C–6, but slightly smoother. Since wollastonite is a natural frit, it melts smoothly like glass and at slightly lower temperatures. If it's used on top of another glaze, the gases boiling off the first glaze will break up the surface of the C6W glaze on top and cause a mottled effect. C6W takes copper and manganese very well and works well in combination with the original C–6 base glaze.

18 has a very waxy surface. It takes oxides very well, but tends to give a flatter, more uniform color. It has no zinc in the base for oxides that are affected by zinc (iron and copper especially). Dolomite and silica replace zinc as the flux.

This will give you an idea of the common glaze materials and how they are used. It gives you ranges and directions to work in. Other materials can be substituted as well. These materials are all nontoxic and easy to work with. Once you get to know about them and get one or two surfaces you like and that take the colorants you want, stick with them.

There are hundreds of glaze recipes. (See Appendix B for some we use.) If you get to know the common materials we've introduced you to here, you'll be able to evaluate and approach recipes you find in other books.

SOME PRACTICAL TIPS

1. *If you don't have a gram scale,* for each percent of most of the coloring oxides indicated in your glaze recipe, try adding 1 teaspoonful of oxide to each dry pound of glaze. For example, if a glaze recipe calls for a 3% addition of copper to the base glaze, use three teaspoons for each pound of *dry* glaze. If your glaze is already mixed with water, there will be about one pound of dry glaze in two pounds of wet glaze. In that case, add one teaspoon of coloring oxide to *two* pounds of wet glaze to equal 1%. This is *very* approximate, but it can be used as a starting point if you don't have a gram scale.

2. *If you change firing temperatures,* for example from cone 04 to cone 6, you don't need to throw out all your old glazes. They can easily be adjusted to mature properly at the higher temperature. (You will need a new clay body to work with, though.) Add clay to raise the maturing temperature. You'll have to run some tests to determine exactly how much to add. *Remember:* Adding clay to a glaze, fired at the same temperature, will make it more matt. By adding clay, you can both raise the maturing temperature and make the surface more matt—but you have to add quite a bit.

You can't really reverse this process. If you decide to fire at cone 04 instead of cone 6, it's easier to reformulate the glaze entirely.

To reduce the maturing temperature of a cone 9 glaze so that it can be fired at cone 6, try replacing about 25% of the feldspar with nepheline syenite, which is a stronger flux. Or you can decrease the clay. To go from cone 6 up to cone 9, add some clay and/or reduce the fluxes.

Changing colemanite and nepheline syenite to feldspar will cause less fluxing action. In other words, if you understand what materials are in your glaze and how they work, you will be able to adjust the maturing temperature up or down slightly.

3. *Granular versus powdered forms of oxides:* Granular rutile or illmenite is used in the clay body for specks. Since you cannot easily convert it to a powdered form, it is best to buy "powdered" rutile or illmenite when a glaze calls for it as a colorant. Have both forms on hand.

FIRING IN YOUR ELECTRIC KILN

Very dry pots of even consistency can be single-fired. However, most potters prefer to double-fire their pots—once before glazing and once after. These two firings are called *bisque-firing* and *glaze-firing.* One reason for firing twice is that green-ware is extremely fragile, and you must be very careful to avoid breakage if you apply glaze or decorate. A second reason for a preliminary bisque-firing is to weed out the potential disasters early. It's far better for a pot to crack, fall apart, or blow up in the bisque kiln. First of all, you haven't put a lot of time and effort into glazing it. Second, glazed pots that explode in a glaze-firing tend to stick together or to other pots, kiln shelves, etc., and become fused in place. They ruin all they come in contact with. However, if you are working primarily with colored clays and engobes and your glazing consists mainly of applying a liner, you may eventually be tempted to single-fire your work. It does save fuel and perhaps time. But you do need to be more careful in handling the ware.

Bisque-Firing. The normal way of bisque-firing for hobby potters is to bisque to a lower temperature than the one at which the clay body matures. This leaves the pots porous for absorbing the glaze. If you are firing your glaze kiln to cone 6, you probably want to bisque-fire at around 08 (900 °C). Manufacturers of china, who want the strength of a clay body fired to a high temperature but want the bright colors of a glaze fired to low temperatures from bisque to maturity (cones 6–12, for example), add a gelatin substance to their glazes to make them adhere to the non-porous bisque-ware and then glaze-fire to a low temperature.

If you are just learning to fire your pots, the most common approach is to bisque low and glaze-fire higher.

Preliminary Steps.

1. *Prepare your kiln shelves by coating them with kilnwash.* Kilnwash is available commercially, or you can make your own. A mixture of half kaolin and half flint combined with water to the thickness of heavy cream works fine. Use it on fire clay shelves (which you will be using if firing to cone 6 or below) or silicon carbide shelves (for higher temperatures). Do not use kilnwash if you are salt glazing (it turns into a glaze). Kilnwash provides an insurance layer between your pots and your kiln shelves. If, by some chance, glaze does run down onto the kilnwash, it will peel the wash off the shelf when you remove it from the kiln. But it won't ruin the kiln shelf by sticking to it.

To apply fresh kilnwash, chip off the old wash first. Dampen your shelves with a wide paint brush dipped in water. Brush on kilnwash and cover thoroughly. Before it dries completely, brush another coat on at right angles to the first. You will probably want a third coat at right angles to the second.

2. *Prepare your cone pats or set the cone in the automatic shut-off.* Pyrometric cones are a necessary part of every potter's supply list. They are small or large, (they come in two sizes) ceramic pyramids that are calibrated to melt at a very specific temperature. The melting temperature varies slightly with the size of the cone and the speed at which the temperature was arrived at. If your electric kiln has an automatic shut-off, and you are firing to cone 08 bisque (cone 6 glaze), simply set the switch with the cone resting between the prongs. When the kiln reaches temperature, the cone begins to melt and lets the top prong down, activating the shut-off switch. This is very convenient because you can leave your studio while the kiln is firing and it will shut itself off at the right temperature.

If you do not have an automatic shut-off, you need to prepare a cone *pat*. Do this ahead of time so the clay can dry. Place it in front of the peep-hole in your kiln so you can see when you should shut your kiln off. Prepare several of them to place in other parts of your kiln. That way when you are unloading the kiln you will have a history of the firing—you'll know if some parts of the kiln were hotter or colder than others. (This works for kilns with automatic shut-offs, too.) You'll be able to match your glazes to the kiln by placing glazes that fire at slightly higher or lower temperatures in the appropriate place in the kiln. Normally, a cone pat consists of three cones, the middle one being the one you fire to. Slant them slightly (8 °) towards the lowest cone so they will bend over in that direction when they melt.

3. *Make sure your pots are completely dry.* The standard test for dryness is to hold a pot against your face. If it still feels cool, it is damp. If your pots have thick walls or you are trying to fire solid pieces of sculpture, give them some extra drying time—at least a week. The best drying atmosphere, at the beginning, is one that is quite warm and high in humidity. If this sounds strange, there's a reason for it. A wall of clay must dry from the inside out. If the air is very dry and the outside of the wall dries completely, the moisture will not be able to escape from the inside of the wall. Later, when trapped water is heated, it forms steam and expands, causing the wall of the pot to burst open. If heavy beginner pots are covered with plastic for awhile to equalize the moisture, dried fairly slowly in a humid atmosphere, then dried to completion, and then fired slowly, accidents are less likely to happen.

If you open your bisque kiln after firing and find that handles have fallen off or bottoms of pots have blown out, the fault was probably not with the bisque-firing, although too rapid an increase at the earlier stages of firing might have encouraged a potential problem to materialize. The problem was probably in the constructing or drying stages, or even earlier, when you wedged the clay.

Other common cracking areas are rims, usually from poorly wedged or overworked clay, or bottoms that are very irregular; the thin areas tend to dry and shrink much more rapidly, which produces stress and cracking. If you begin throwing pots off the hump, a common cracking problem is known as the "S" crack. There are a number of reasons for this as well, but you can cure the problem by taking special care to "compact" the clay in the bottom of hump-thrown pots (Fig. 12-8).

Fig. 12-8 Cracking of a wide form.

Many cracking problems will disappear automatically as your skill in working with clay improves: Wedging properly, throwing confidently and directly, constructing carefully, trimming evenly, handling pots properly. The abuse a beginner gives the clay in the earlier stages often does not take its toll until the pot has been bisque-fired or even glaze-fired.

Stacking the Bisque Kiln. In a small kiln with only a few pieces of ware, you really don't need to worry too much about stacking efficiently. Put all the pots in— the same height pots on the first shelf, if possible. (This shelf should be 2 inches or so above the floor of the kiln. Never stack directly on the floor.) Put three posts on the edges in a triangular pattern to support the next shelf (making sure the posts are higher than the pots as in Fig. 12-9). Put the next shelf in, and load the rest of your pots on that. That's probably all the room you'll have in a small kiln.

If you are stacking a larger kiln or have more ware, you may want to worry about efficiency. If you stack pots inside each other (Fig. 12-10), you'll be able to load more in the kiln. Actually, a full kiln

Fig. 12-9 Measuring pot height relative to post height.

Fig. 12-10 Stacking pots inside each other (bisque).

tends to fire more evenly than a partially stacked one (Fig. 12–11). If you are really "loaded down," though, it will take a longer firing time to drive off all the water and heat up the additional ware. If you do fire pots one inside another, here are some things to remember:

1. Their foot rims should coincide.
2. Don't place a heavy pot on a delicate one.
3. Leave enough space between walls for expansion.
4. Stack mugs rim to rim.
5. Stack small pots rim to rim inside larger pots, but be careful.
6. Fire pots which have lids with the lid *on* to prevent warping. The lid can be turned upside down with the knob inside to save space.

Fig. 12-11 Partially stacked bisque kiln.

The Bisque-Firing Schedule. Firing is a gradual heating and gradual cooling process, each of equal duration, (except in the case of Raku). In a small electric kiln, an eight- or ten-hour period of time to get up to temperature, plus an equal time to cool, is normal. If you have a pyrometer, you will know how fast your kiln temperature is climbing and what stage your pots are going through.

At lower temperatures, it is important to leave the door of the kiln open so water can evaporate out and so the temperature rise is gradual. Even though your pots feel bone dry, there is still some physical water in the clay until they're fired to about 200°C. Just as with drying, the water should be driven off slowly from the inside of the wall out. As a precaution, we usually leave the bisque kiln on low overnight for heavy pots or student work. Plan on at least four hours before you let your kiln climb above 200°C.

There is also what is known as "chemical" water in clay. The formula for clay, theoretically, is $Al_2O_3 \cdot 2SiO_2 \cdot 2H_2O$. This means that there is approximately one pound of water (chemically combined with the alumina and silica) for every eight pounds of clay. So even after the pots are free of all physical water, the kiln door should remain slightly ajar to burn this chemical water off. A 150°C–200°C an hour rise in temperature after 200°C is reasonable. By watching your pyrometer and adjusting your switches, you can easily control this. If you do not have a pyrometer, you should plan on turning up your switches very gradually. Keep the door ajar up to about 600°C. Since the top of

an electric kiln tends to get hotter than the bottom, it's a good idea to always turn up the bottom switch before the top. This will help equalize the temperature.

Glaze-Firing. Glaze-firing is just like bisque-firing, really. The main difference is that you fire to a higher temperature and cannot let the glazed surfaces of the pots touch each other or the kiln shelves.

If you are stacking beginner pots in a glaze kiln, make sure your shelves are thoroughly kilnwashed. Otherwise you risk ruining the shelves if any glaze runs onto them. If you are testing glazes (you should try a few tests in each glaze kiln you fire), a good precaution is to put all the test tiles or mites on an old piece of bisque-ware to catch any glaze that runs more than you think it will.

Normally, you will "dry-foot" your pots

Fig. 12-12 Wiping pots for "dry-footing."

Fig. 12-13 Wiping slightly for stilting.

—fire them flat on the kiln shelf, bottoms free of glaze (Fig. 12–12). Some pots can be placed on "stilts" (wipe as in Fig. 12–13), if you want to cover them with glaze on all sides. Wide-bottomed pieces, like plates, should *not* be stilted. No pot should hang over the edge of the shelf. It could warp or slump.

It's a good idea to keep a time–temperature log of each firing. (It's also a good idea to keep a glaze notebook with comments on the results of each firing.) This will help you remember what you have done before so you can make adjustments later. It will also help you analyze your results. You'll realize if your kiln is taking a long time to reach temperature that you might have a burned-out element or a faulty switch.

Slow Cooling. Taking a very hot pot out of the kiln is not a good idea. Both dunting and crazing are likely to occur. But remember, if you cool your kiln too rapidly by opening the door too soon, you risk damaging the refractories (shelves, firebrick, etc.). Cool slowly until you can handle the pots inside comfortably with bare hands. This is more important than seeing your pots right away.

If the kiln shuts off before it reaches temperature, you *can* refire your pots. This may happen if the timer shuts the kiln off before the cone melts. When you refire, use a *new cone*. The original cone may have crystallized on cooling and will not melt at the same temperature the second time.

Caution. Don't try "reduction" in an electric kiln. Almost anything that will produce a reducing atmosphere will also "reduce" the elements in your kiln. It will shorten their lives considerably. We hear

Fig. 12-14 Animal; Hans Warta. Clay, stain, cone 6 oxidation. (*Courtesy of the artist*)

people talk about things they have heard or read about doing to an electric kiln— throwing mothballs in, putting Bunsen burners in the peephole, throwing in pine needles soaked in machine oil, etc. This may be effective as far as producing a reducing atmosphere for your pots, but it's not too smart as far as the life of your kiln elements is concerned.

Localized reduction, such as that produced by silicon carbide as a component of the glaze, will not damage kiln elements and is potentially a good technique. There is a danger of glaze defects, though, resulting from this method—pitting or pinholing in the surface of the glaze.

If you are firing in an electric kiln, *accept the oxidation atmosphere, and work within it.* Don't try to imitate a gas kiln.

Note Figs. 12–14 through 12–23, gallery photographs that may give you some ideas.

Fig. 12-15 Candlestick pair; Barbara Sexton. Handbuilt slab with contrasting colored clays, cone 04 oxidation. (*Courtesy of the artist*) (*Photo by L. Wicklund*)

Fig. 12-16 Covered jar; Leif Wicklund. Colored clay overlay, cone 04 oxidation. (*Courtesy the artist*)

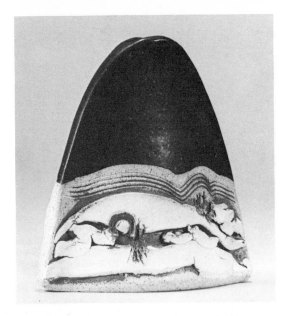

Fig. 12-17 Slab construction; Rick and Eileen Schlag. White clay appliqued to buff body with black glaze and strain accents. This particular pot was fired at cone 10 reduction, but similar effects can be achieved in oxidation. (*Courtesy of the artists*)

Fig. 12-18 "Doe Boy (USA)"; Garry Sherman. Handbuilt and wheel-thrown. (*Courtesy of the artist*)

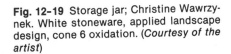

Fig. 12-19 Storage jar; Christine Wawrzynek. White stoneware, applied landscape design, cone 6 oxidation. (*Courtesy of the artist*)

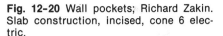

Fig. 12-20 Wall pockets; Richard Zakin. Slab construction, incised, cone 6 electric.

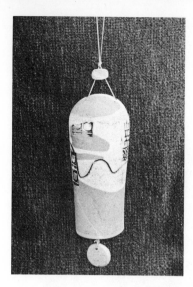

Fig. 12-21 Bell; Richard Zakin. Stamped and incised colored clay with stain, cone 6 electric. (*Courtesy of the artist*)

Fig. 12-22 Dragon covered jar; Pat Probst Gilman. Cone 12-14 porcelain, incised design. (*Courtesy of the artist*) (*Photo by Ruth Pasquine*)

136

TROUBLESHOOTING AFTER OPENING A KILN: GLAZE DEFECTS

Matt Glazes Versus Shiny Glazes. Matt glazes are more susceptible to surface defects than shiny ones. In the case of matt glaze defects, the basic problem is that a matt glaze does not flow at its highest temperature. In other words, the surface tension remains high, and holes, bare spots, or irregularities of thickness remain the same or in some instances are exaggerated. In a shinier glaze, these irregularities all melt together and smooth out. The evenness which makes a shiny glaze surface seem less varied or less interesting also makes it much easier to work with. (In other words, there's no way of curing the problem without killing the patient.)

The other problem with a matt glaze is that it may still be immature—not fired quite high enough. There is usually a very narrow temperature range of acceptability with an immature matt glaze. If fired just a little too low, the surface will be too dry, almost like the clay body; if fired just a little too high, the surface will become shiny (reach maturity actually). A shiny glaze normally has a broader firing range than a matt glaze. This narrow range, in the case of matt glazes, plus its greater susceptibility to application errors, make these glazes harder for the beginner to control than shiny ones.

Matt Glazes. These are particularly susceptible to *crawling*—a surface which looks as if the clay has balled up in blotches leaving unglazed clay showing around the

137

patches of glaze—and *pinholing (or pitting)*, little holes in the glaze surface. Matt glazes, in general, have less tolerance for application irregularities or firing inconsistencies than shiny glazes.

Shiny Glazes. These glazes, on the other hand, are susceptible to *crazing*—the crackling in the surface that occurs because "the glaze is too small for the area over which it is stretched and therefore breaks like a splitting seam in a too small pair of trousers." (Rhodes, *Clay and Glazes*, p. 153.) Shiny glazes are occasionally susceptible to *shivering,* which is the opposite of crazing, the glaze being too big for the clay and buckling like a sidewalk. Both are due to improper fit between the glaze and the clay body.

Shrinkage and Its Relationship to Crazing and Crawling. In talking about matt and shiny glaze defects, people talk about two *very different* types of shrinkage. *One* type of shrinkage (that related to crawling) occurs as a glaze *dries* on the pot it has been applied to—before it is ever fired. Since glaze has clay in it, it dries and shrinks much the same way as a freshly thrown pot. If there is too much clay in the glaze or the drying is forced too rapidly, the clay will shrink and tend to pull apart. The crawling probably will not be evident until after you have fired the pot.

The *second* type of shrinkage (that associated with crazing) is due to contraction during the cooling cycle of the *firing.* The usual problem is that the glaze contracts more than the clay pot it covers, since the flux materials of the glaze tend to shrink more than the clay materials of the body. This is crazing. If the glaze should shrink less than the body upon cooling, a much less-common occurrence, you may get *shivering.* The glaze may pop right off the pot.

THE MOST COMMON GLAZE PROBLEMS AND THEIR CURES

The cause of most glaze defects can be found in:

1. The clay body composition,
2. the base glaze composition,
3. the application of glaze to ware, or
4. the firing.

Do not look to the glaze alone as the cause of the problem. It is often a combination of problems requiring adjustment of one or more of these four areas.

Too Shiny, Runny, or Dry a Glaze Surface. *If your glaze surface is too shiny:*
• You might have over-fired your kiln, or this pot might have been in a hot spot. Check the cones.
• If the firing was normal, you can either *decrease* some of the flux (if you are mixing up your own glaze recipe) or *add* some clay (if you're doctoring commercial glazes).
• If you like the surface but are having trouble with the glaze running onto kiln shelves, make sure you have wiped and feathered far enough up the side of the pot.
• In the case of a crystalline matt glaze firing too shiny, a longer cooling cycle will give the crystals more time to grow. The crystals which develop in the surface are what make it matt. (This is the other type of matt glaze, as opposed to the immature surface.)
• If some of your glaze materials come in very fine-particled sizes, this may be making a matt or satin glaze a little shiny. Smaller particle sizes will reduce the maturing temperature of a glaze.
If the glaze surface is too dry:
• You may have underfired your kiln, or the pot may have been in a cold spot.
• If you're sure temperature is not the

problem, add more flux to your glaze (colemanite, zinc, feldspar, talc, a frit, etc.). Or, if you are mixing the glazes yourself, decrease the clay.

• It's also possible that the glaze was too thinly applied, and the surface of the clay is basically unglazed.

Crawling. If crawling is your problem, it means that for some reason the glaze wasn't thoroughly attached to the pot before the firing began (see Shrinkage and Its Relationship to Crazing and Crawling, p. 138). Here are some causes and remedies for crawling:

1. The glaze formula may need adjusting: The glaze may have too much clay in it or too fine-particled a clay. Switch from ball clay to kaolin as a first step if you are using ball clay. Or use less clay. However, you may also lose your matt surface as well as the crawling problem if you decrease the clay content much.

• Colemanite or another flocculant in your glaze base can be a problem. A flocculant thickens your glaze (almost like adding flour or cornstarch to gravy), and too thick an application of glaze will lead to crawling.

2. The glaze may be applied improperly:

• Too thick an application.

• Glaze applied on dusty or greasy pots. Wipe off pots that have been sitting around for a while before you glaze them.

• Sometimes double-dipping a pot in glaze.

3. Firing procedures may cause crawling:

• Loading pots into the kiln while the glaze is still wet and firing immediately (a very *common cause* of crawling).

• Firing the kiln with the door closed from the beginning, not giving the water in the glaze a chance to escape.

If crawling is your problem, it usually has to do with a clay–water ratio and the drying and shrinking of the glaze on the bisqueware before the firing begins. In the case of either crawling or pinholing (which follows), a good precautionary measure is to wait until the glaze dries; then, just before you stack the kiln, rub your hand on the surface of the glaze, smoothing out holes and irregularities.

Pinholing and Pitting. These are annoying, difficult to cure, and the second major problem with matt glazes. When any glaze is fired, the volatile materials boil and burn off at higher temperatures. What usually is occurring in the case of pinholing is that the bubbles in the boiling glaze are somehow being solidified in the glaze's surface and are not given a chance to smooth out—usually this is caused by too rapid a cooling cycle. Here are some things to try if you have pinholes in your fired glazes:

1. Lengthen your firing cycle; soak your kiln at the top temperature; cool more slowly.

2. Add a little more flux to your glaze or fire to a slightly higher temperature.

3. Cut back on zinc and rutile—these materials tend to contribute to pinholing. Cut back on carbonates (whiting) and clay materials that volatilize at the higher temperatures.

4. In reduction firing, body-reduce less. The carbon deposited at the earlier stages of body reduction will volatilize as CO_2 later on, and the gas burning out through the glaze from the body may be contributing to the pinholing.

Crazing. If the glaze contracts more than the clay body on cooling and a network of fine cracks develops, crazing has occurred (see Shrinkage and Its Relationship to Crazing and Crawling, p. 138).

The fluxes sodium and potassium produce the greatest firing shrinkage. Try to replace these fluxes (partly) with whiting or dolomite (at cone 6 and higher), which shrink less. You can also try decreasing the flux in your glaze; this may prevent the crazing but may produce a more matt surface than you want.

Probably the most successful cure is to substitute silica for some of the flux. Silica is the glass former in your glaze, so it will tend to keep the glaze shiny; but it also has a low thermal expansion—lower than the fluxes.

Oddly enough, if you are mixing up your own clay, silica can also be added to the clay to correct the same problem. It works quite differently in the clay body, staying in its crystalline form, quartz. As the clay body cools, what is known as a *quartz inversion* takes place at 573 °C; the quartz contracts, causing the clay body to shrink slightly. Too much silica in the clay body may lead to other problems which produce cracking, however. The best solution to crazing is to add the silica to the glaze.

Shivering. This is the opposite of crazing— a wrong fit in reverse, the clay body shrinking *more* than the glaze. This is much less common but can be cured, reasonably enough, by reversing the solutions to crazing. Basically, if you have a shivering problem, try adding fluxes to the glaze or decreasing the silica in the clay body.

Spit-outs in a Finished Pot. These can occur from foreign matter in the clay body. One common contaminant is plaster from bats. Contamination from a number of sources is more likely to happen when you use reclaimed clay. Other potential trouble-makers are: vermiculite (pyrometric cones come packed in it) and small pieces of sponge or chamois. You probably picked them up from the wedging table when you wedged the clay. They will burn out during firing and cause craters or cracks in the finished pot.

Another source of spit-outs might be in the original clay from the manufacturer. One major manufacturer recently distributed fire clay with impurities that caused black spit-outs in the glazed surface.

This "problem" of foreign matter burning out during firing can, under controlled conditions, be used constructively for special effects. An example—Chinese rice bowls that have rice embedded in the porcelain clay before firing. The rice burns off and leaves a very irregular textural pattern and different degrees of translucency.

Examine glaze "defects" carefully for any positive potential as well as analyzing their causes with the intent to cure them.

Getting in a Little Further

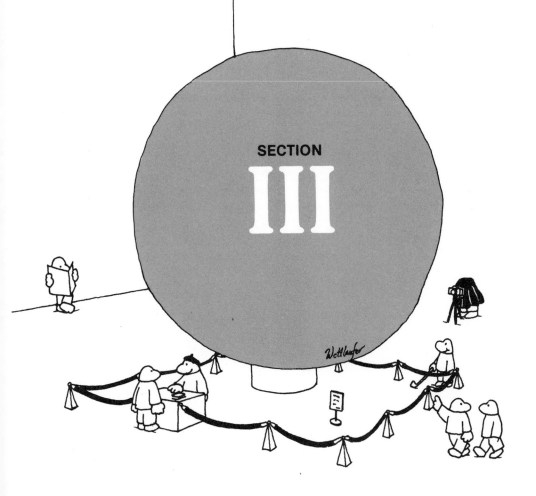

SECTION

III

CHAPTER **13**

Gas
Kilns

We encouraged beginners and hobby potters to learn to fire in an electric kiln in Section II. In many cases, this may be the only kiln you will ever need or want. If you are mixing your own glazes, have already learned to fire an electric kiln, are making a substantial number of pots, and have a permanent studio set-up, you may want to consider a gas kiln. This chapter is divided into three parts. The first part deals with buying or building gas kilns; the second part gives our own gas-kiln firing method which will help you control reduction; and the third part describes some reliable cone 10 reduction glazes. Glazing and firing in the gas kiln are more difficult than building it.

BUILDING OR BUYING A GAS KILN

First of all, do some reading before you make any final decisions. Both Dan Rhodes' and Fred Olsen's books on kilns contain valuable information (see Bibliography for details). If you can get hold of the Summer '73 issue of *Studio Potter,* it also has some good information on kiln design. If you are thinking of building your own gas kiln, which is probably the best idea, you may also want to begin contacting suppliers for price lists of burners and refractories, especially shelves. Here are some things to consider in deciding whether to build or buy as well as what size kiln is best for you.

Our Arguments Against a Small Gas Kiln.
If you are a low-volume potter, we recommend firing in a small electric kiln for ease and consistency. An electric kiln has elements throughout, so the heat distribution is no real problem to control. A fuel burning kiln, on the other hand, introduces a fluid-flow problem. You put heat in with burners at one point and, by means of a draft, draw it through the kiln as evenly as possible and out the other end. This requires skill.

Do not make the mistake of thinking that a small gas kiln will be easier to control than a large gas kiln. It is somewhat analogous to sailing a small versus a large sailboat—the smaller are much trickier to control. Both their smaller size and their updraft flue system make small gas kilns very touchy.

A Brief Explanation of "Updraft" and "Downdraft." An *updraft kiln* has an opening in the top. It has no chimney. Heat goes into the kiln at the base by means of burners and goes out through the top. The standard problem with this type of kiln is that the bottom part of the kiln tends to fire hotter than the top part. Unfortunately, the updraft system is the simplest and takes the least amount of space. This is why it is used in smaller, less expensive kilns.

A *downdraft* system, on the other hand, has a flue opening in the lower part of the kiln which leads into a stack or chimney. Heat going into the kiln at the base rises to the top and is pulled back down to the bottom again. This produces more even circulation of heat and gases. But this design is more feasible in a large kiln.

An *up-down* system is similar to the downdraft but with an additional flue opening into the stack at the top of the kiln. This is the design we use.

Types of Small Gas Kilns. Although we do not recommend firing in a small gas kiln, there are many on the market and also many do-it-yourself options. Some are easier to build or less expensive than others, but all of them are difficult to fire with much consistency—especially if you have no prior experience firing gas kilns.

There are castable refractories which can be poured or molded. You can build your own small kiln out of these.

There are Fiber-frax (insulating) blankets with which you can line a 55-gallon drum. This makes a better Raku kiln than a stoneware kiln.

You can convert an old electric kiln to a gas kiln by putting a hole in the bottom for a burner and putting a hole in the top for a draft.

You can buy a small gas kiln for $500 or under. For insulating material, the kiln might use any of the above.

If you are considering buying a small gas kiln, ask the distributor for names of potters who own them, and check with one or two of them about performance and durability.

The Kiln We Recommend. Our advice is that you build a gas kiln that has close to a 10-cubic-foot capacity or more. We have included here some photos and drawings of our 30-cubic-foot gas kiln and an explanation of how to adapt it to the 10-cubic-foot size range.

Our kiln has an up-down draft design (Figs. 13–1 and 13–2). It has flue openings in the back, both top and bottom, which lead into the chimney, or stack, on the back of the kiln. The roof of the kiln is flat,

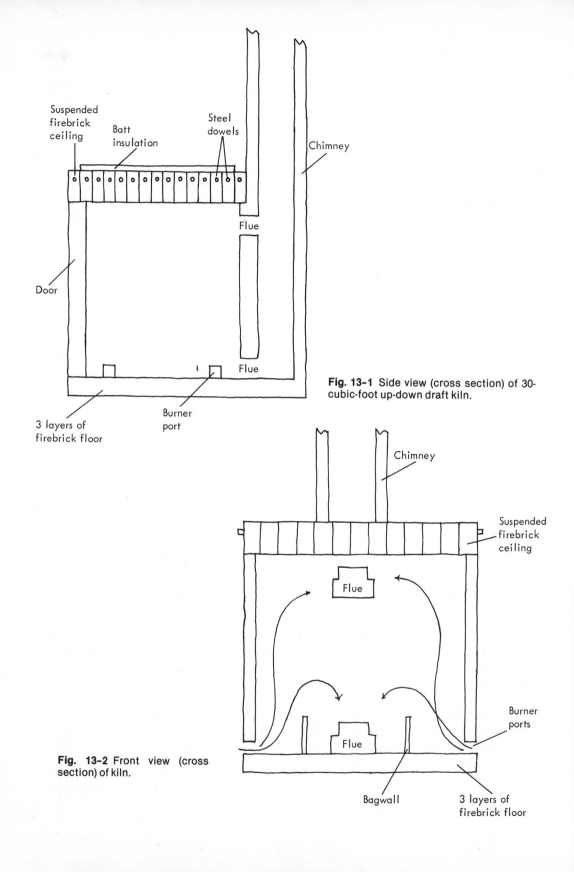

Suspended firebrick ceiling

Batt insulation

Steel dowels

Chimney

Flue

Door

Flue

Flue

3 layers of firebrick floor

Burner port

Fig. 13-1 Side view (cross section) of 30-cubic-foot up-down draft kiln.

Chimney

Suspended firebrick ceiling

Flue

Flue

Burner ports

Bagwall

3 layers of firebrick floor

Fig. 13-2 Front view (cross section) of kiln.

constructed from insulating firebrick suspended on ¾-inch cold-rolled steel rods. The kiln is basically a cube, a little taller than it is wide. (See Rhodes, p. 114.) There are four burner ports, two in either side. (See Fig. 13-3.) The door is in front, and we rebuild it each time to close the kiln after stacking it.

The 10-cubic-foot design is similar. However, you will only need two burners to heat the smaller kiln, and these can enter through the front.

We chose the up-down draft system for control purposes. If the top of the kiln gets too hot during firing, the bottom flue can be opened wider to draw more heat back down into the bottom of the kiln. If heat builds up in the bottom and the top is cool, the bottom opening can be closed some and the top opened more to draw the heat and gases up to the top. The problem most potters firing gas kilns have is getting heat and gases evenly distributed to all parts of the kiln. We are able to achieve excellent results using this up-down combination draft system, and it has the advantage of being adjustable even during firing.

Materials Needed to Build a 10-Cubic-Foot Gas Kiln. The main factor in determining the exact dimensions of the kiln you will build is the size kiln shelves you can get (and lift). For firing to stoneware temperatures, you will need silicon carbide shelves. These are available from most pottery suppliers but are relatively expensive. For ⅝-inch thick slabs, you can expect to pay about $15.00 a square foot. A shopping list follows for the materials you will need to build a 10-cubic-foot kiln of our design.

You can see that the materials alone will cost close to $750 for this kiln. Why is it that you can buy a commercially made gas kiln of almost the same size for less than $500? Because of the design of our kiln, which requires an outside chimney built from costly firebrick. Since this design, however, will give better firing results, the initial extra expense will pay for itself shortly. If you were to build your own kiln with the same design as the commercially made kiln, it would probably cost you about the same amount of money.

The following shopping list combined with the photos and line drawings of our kiln should help you start planning your kiln. Before you actually begin construction, you should consult Rhodes or Olsen for more specifics.

Whether you buy or build a gas kiln, you will need a shelter of some kind—don't build a gas kiln in a wood structure. (See Fig. 13-4.) The $200, 10' × 10' metal garden sheds available from Sears, etc, work well, especially if you pour a concrete slab first. The kind with plastic panes in the roof also give you light while you're stacking.

Fig. 13-3 Flames entering rear burner fire boxes.

1. *Silicon Carbide Shelves* (10–12 @ $12–$15)................$150.00
   If you use 8″ × 16″ shelves, kiln size might be:
   > 27 × 18 × 30 inches (inside)......or 8½ cu ft.
   > or   27 × 18 × 36 inches.............. 10 cu ft.

2. *500 Firebrick* (K–23, @ $.60)..........................$300.00
   Approximate distribution of firebrick:

sides	200
bottom	72
top	84
flue	84

   K–23 Brick withstands 2350°F temperatures. The insulating properties of these are twice as good as for K–26's, which will fire to a higher temperature (cone 10 is about 2350°F—the maximum temperature for K–23 bricks). With the better insulating properties of the K–23's, which we use without any problem and recommend, you end up losing less heat and saving fuel and money for each firing.

   Caution: If someone is giving you brick or you have a scrounge source somewhere, make *sure* the brick has the proper insulating qualities for the temperature you're firing to. Even a firebrick becomes a glaze if fired too high.

3. *Burners* (for this size kiln, 2 are enough; @ $50.00).........$100.00
   We use Ransome, R.U.T. Burners. Different types vary in price—see *Studio Potter,* Summer '73, for different manufacturers of burners (and safety systems), with addresses. Also check your local industrial supply house for burners.

4. *Miscellaneous* $100.00
   ¾″ steel rod, 8″ & 12″ metal flue piping, angle iron, kiln furniture (posts), etc.

5. *Optional But Highly Recommended* $75.00
   A gas analyzer (see next section on reduction firing, p. 149)—to measure amount of reduction. You will also need a quartz tube.
   A pyrometer to measure temperature.

Fig. 13-4 Installing chimney.

FIRING A GAS KILN

A Method of Monitoring and Controlling Reduction.

No potter would wish to preclude all accidents, happy or otherwise, from his work, but there are ways of setting the stage for the happy accident. It is frequently observed that the happiest accidents always occur in the work of the potter who is capable of allowing no accidents to happen if he so desires.
(Dan Rhodes, *Stoneware and Porcelain,* p. 212.

The difficult thing about reduction firing is that it is hard to tell exactly how much the kiln is reducing. Meters are now available to determine and to record the amount of carbon monoxide in the kiln or flue—these meters are too expensive and complex to come into general use in studio potteries.
(Dan Rhodes, *Clay and Glazes,* p. 180.)

Since 1965 when *Clay and Glazes* was written, such meters have been made available to the studio potter or to the teaching potter at reasonable prices. But most potters are still unaware that they exist. Instead of a carbon monoxide analyzer, as mentioned by Rhodes, we use one which measures carbon dioxide, an equally (or more) effective indicator, as will be explained shortly. Ours is called a Fyrite Gas Analyzer. It works on the Orsat method of measuring gas, and it is manufactured by Bacharach Industrial Instrument Co. (see Appendix A, Suppliers). They are available at about $75.00 from most oil burner supply places and are simple to use. In fact, most oil burner repairmen coming to clean your home furnace will use one to check its efficiency.

Using an analyzer while firing your kiln also serves the dual purpose of helping you to conserve fuel by firing efficiently and allowing you to monitor and control the amount of reduction in the kiln's atmosphere. We estimate that since we have been using the analyzer, we have cut back at least 20% on fuel consumption, a real financial saving.

Few studio potters can afford the costly trial-and-error process often involved in getting the feel of firing each individual kiln (although firing will always be an art as well as a science). Several experienced studio potters have told us that it took them at least six firings to zero in on the proper amount of reduction for their glazes. In modest terms, this probably cost between one and two thousand dollars in wasted ware and fuel, not to mention the discouragement over losing that much time and effort. A studio potter supporting a family cannot afford that kind of loss, and if he should change fuels or build a new kiln, the process starts again. (See Fig. 13–5.)

Since we have been using the analyzer, we have switched kilns (both to different sizes and different shapes) three times; always having recorded sample gas data from the previous kiln. We never have had a disastrously bad firing. If the first firing in a new kiln was slightly off, we knew what direction to go to correct it. After that we were able to maintain consistently adequate amounts of reduction regularly for our glazes (which are particularly sensitive in this respect). Having near zero losses due to firing is critical when financial survival is at stake. This does not mean that we're not eager to open each new kiln—there are always surprises. And if an interesting kiln

accident should occur, we usually have enough data on the firing to reproduce it (Fig. 13-6).

Inadequacies in Written Glaze Recipes. Besides decreasing losses, use of the gas analyzer will make it possible for potters to be more precise about glaze communications. At present, glazes describe the raw materials in the formula, the firing temperature, and whether fired in oxidation or reduction. In the future, if potters begin using the gas analyzer, "reduction" will be described quantitatively, and *how much* reduction will become part of the glaze recipe. Sample glaze instructions might read: "Fire at 10% carbon dioxide for five hours between cone 1 and cone 10."

Fig. 13-5 Glaze kiln stacked and ready to fire.

Fig. 13-6 Pots with same glaze fired to same temperature showing varying amounts of reduction—three different firings.

Specific numerical indications of *both* temperature and atmosphere and the relationship between the two over a period of time will become possible and should be very helpful.

There are other variables that affect the quality of fired glazes. Fewer than half of these are normally described in written glaze recipes. We are mainly talking about atmosphere here, but there are other things to consider. While glaze recipes normally include the raw materials necessary, they omit mention of particle size. Finely ground particles will decrease the maturing temperature of the glaze by as much as 50°C. The purity of the raw materials may also vary according to the whims of nature or the manufacturer. Written glaze recipes may also omit any indication of how thick to mix up a glaze or apply it to a pot.

Glaze recipes include a firing temperature but omit mention of time or of the heating-cooling cycle. They indicate atmosphere (oxidation or reduction) but never how much over what period of time at what temperatures. Water in the atmosphere is never mentioned, and this can be influential. Also omitted is a description of the clay body the glaze is being applied to. Both its color and density will affect the color of the glaze as well as how it "fits" the pot and its surface quality. With this in mind, let's return to the one variable atmosphere.

What is Reduction? First of all, what is combustion? It is the result of combining air and fuel (in our case propane). Fuels are a combination of hydrogen and carbon —propane is C_3H_8. When combined with oxygen in combustion, it yields water and carbon dioxide.

$$C_3H_8 + 5O_2 \longrightarrow 3CO_2 + 4H_2O$$

When the proportion of oxygen exceeds that of fuel, the result is an oxidizing atmosphere—the byproducts of combustion being water and carbon dioxide, as shown above, plus extra oxygen. When the ratio of fuel to oxygen is greater, the result is a reducing atmosphere.

In reduction, the byproducts of combustion will be carbon dioxide and water, less than before, plus very active hydrogen and carbon monoxide molecules looking for more oxygen so they can return to their more stable state of water and carbon dioxide. The higher the temperature, the more active the hydrogen and carbon monoxide molecules become in their search for oxygen. When they cannot find it in the oxygen-starved atmosphere of the kiln, they will obtain it by attacking the oxides in the clay and glazes. These in turn are more willing to give up their oxygen at a higher temperature. This chemical reaction of extracting the oxygen molecule from the oxides in the clay and glazes is called *reduction.*

While it was previously assumed that carbon monoxide was the only reducing agent, it has been shown (by Koenig and others) that the hydrogen molecule is even more effective at attacking the body and glazes. (Reduction is actually determined by the ratios of CO to CO_2 and H_2 to H_2O.)

As the carbon dioxide decreases in the kiln's reducing atmosphere, the carbon monoxide and hydrogen will be increasing proportionately (see Fig. 13-7). The advantage of using CO_2 as the indicator gas is that it is present both in oxidation and reduction and as a result will help you find your most efficient firing point (the centerline in the graph or theoretical neutral), helping both in fuel conservation and control of reduction.

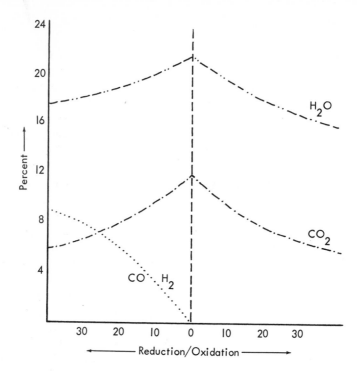

Fig. 13-7 Measuring carbon dioxide to indicate reduction, neutral, and oxidation atmosphere.

What is a CO₂ Analyzer and How Does It Work? A potter inserts a quartz tube through a small hole in the firebrick toward the interior of his kiln and pumps a rubber ball (like a blood-pressure pump) about 20–25 times to draw out a sample of the kiln's atmosphere. (This is called "pumping up the kiln" by 5½-year-old Kurt Wettlaufer.) See Fig. 13-8. The gas sample is sucked into a glass tube containing a chemical (potassium hydroxide) which absorbs the carbon dioxide and expands as a result. The increase in volume causes the fluid to rise in the glass tube whose numbered scale indicates the percentage of carbon dioxide present in your kiln's atmosphere at the time you take the sample. As you can see from Fig. 13-7, a number (8% for example) can occur either in reduction or oxidation. Which side of neutral

(maximum CO_2) you are on is not difficult to determine.

In using an analyzer, the first thing you should try to determine is the maximum percent of CO_2 possible, or neutral. This is theoretically perfect combustion (the peak on the graph) requiring the least amount of fuel and giving off zero pollution in the form of carbon monoxide. To do this, set your kiln so that plenty of air (excess air) is entering the kiln and you are sure that you have an oxidizing atmosphere. Then start gradually closing down the amount of oxygen entering the kiln (closing off both flue and burner openings). Each time you do this, after waiting a few minutes for the kiln's atmosphere to stabilize, take a gas sample. You should be reading progressively higher numbers on the analyzer scale. When the numbers begin to decrease, you know that you have reached neutral and started into reduction. For maximum efficiency, set your flue and burners so that your analyzer gives a reading just slightly lower than the maximum number on the oxidizing side of the scale.

How We Fire Our Propane-Burning Kiln (Using the CO₂ Analyzer). When glaze-firing, from cold up to 1000 °C (about cone 06), we set the kiln for maximum fuel efficiency as described above (see Fig. 13-9)—a reading of about 11–12% or just slightly oxidizing. From 1000 °C to 1050 °C (cone 06 to cone 04), we reduce the clay body. We decrease the air supply until the analyzer records about 8% carbon dioxide, fairly heavy reduction. Remember that as the numbers are decreasing, the amount of reduction is increasing. This takes about an hour. 1050 °C is the point at which our

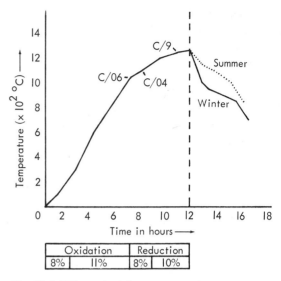

Fig. 13-9 Firing schedule.

Oxidation		Reduction	
8%	11%	8%	10%

Fig. 13-8 Quartz tube inserted into kiln.

glazes begin to fuse, and it is here that we begin a lighter reduction, measuring about 10% CO₂ on the analyzer. We hold this reading until the kiln gets up to temperature, about 4½ more hours.

Note: When and how much body reduction is a function of clay porosity at a given temperature and the amount of iron in the body. You may want to begin body reduction slightly earlier, or you may want to vary the amount of body reduction to suit your glazes.

When bisque-firing in our gas kiln, we maintain an oxidizing atmosphere, reading about 9% on the oxidizing side of the scale, until the carbon burns out of the body—or up to about 700 °C; then we go to almost complete efficiency, or 12% oxidizing, for the remainder of the bisque-firing.

One consideration to keep in mind is the balance between the flue and the burners. We try to maintain a 5–6 ′ per second gas flow through the kiln during oxidation and about 3–4 ′ per second flow during reduction. This is done by closing off the flue and adjusting the burners in proportion to each other—it takes some experimentation. (The oily rag method described by Olsen works well for measuring this.) The settings will vary slightly depending on the *weather* (change in atmospheric pressure outside the kiln.) If wind is a problem in maintaining atmosphere or gas flow, it can be adjusted for by installing an atmospheric damper in the flue, such as those commonly found in oil burner flues. Too strong a draft tends to cause irregular temperatures and to make the kiln overly responsive to wind changes (similar to a sailboat again). Not enough draft may result in too much reduction.

Weather may have other effects on firing. We have mentioned atmospheric pressure. (Firing on a clear day gives a different draft pattern than on an overcast day.) We have also talked about wind, which may give an irregular draft. Both will affect the kiln's atmosphere. Humidity will also tend to give a different reading on the gas analyzer.

Cold weather will also affect the cooling rate. Normally, upon shutting off our kiln, the temperature drops about 100°C, and the atmosphere returns to neutral almost immediately (even with the flue and burner holes blocked up). If the initial temperature drop is more rapid, and it may be in winter, the surface of our glazes tends to become more crystalline. It is possible to run a neutral flame for a few minutes to compensate for the colder weather, allowing the kiln to cool more slowly—more like the summer cooling curve.

Generally, in a firing cycle, what happens on the way up with temperature and atmosphere is reflected on the way down in a mirror image way—almost like a balancing scale. The amount of reduction during firing influences the amount of reoxidation on cooling. Much color development takes place during cooling. If you assume that normally, the cooling half of the process is constant, you can adjust the heating half accordingly. The other thing to keep in mind is that the chemical reactions between gasses and oxides will be the most extreme at the higher temperatures.

The CO_2 Analyzer as a Teaching Device. We have discussed the gas analyzer's usefulness mainly in terms of studio pottery conditions because we are studio potters. Recently we discovered how dramatic the instrument was as a teaching device. We had been invited to demonstrate the use of the analyzer to ceramic students and teachers at a nearby university. We had the instructors set the flue of an updraft kiln for reduction the way they normally did while firing this particular kiln. (Neither agreed exactly how it should be fired—both agreed it was an impossible kiln to fire consistently.) With flames shooting out the top flue, normally an indication of reduction, we played around with the air at the burners and achieved a range of CO_2 readings from neutral to heavy reduction. (The kiln continued to *look* the same.) As we adjusted burners and flue to get from excess air to just under neutral (the highest number on the analyzer scale) and then continued to change kiln settings until we got a number for reduction, the students were amazed and fascinated. They could actually "see" what was happening to the atmosphere inside the kiln.

As teachers discover this, a gas analyzer may become as frequent and as important a piece of kiln equipment as is a pyrometer (or cones) at present. They are equally useful measuring devices: One measures atmosphere, the other temperature—the two critical factors in reduction firing.

GAS KILN GLAZES

In this final section, we describe the glaze formulas that we use in our studio production: Two matt glazes, a shiny liner glaze, and an ash glaze are all that we find necessary (although we do continue to experiment with new glazes and combinations in each kiln that we fire). We have also included some comments about altering and adjusting glaze recipes, which may help you in adapting these to your own particular circumstances. All are reduction-fired as described in the second part of this chapter.

Cone 10 Reduction Glazes. *Two Stoneware Matt Glazes:*

WETTLAUFER BASE (Matt or Waxy Matt Surface)

Spar (C-6, a soda spar)	45
Dolomite	25
Ball Clay	25
Nepheline Syenite	10
Whiting	5

The following oxide additions work well: For a rust to white, add 4% tin oxide; for a blue-brown, add 4% tin oxide plus ¾% cobalt; for a rich gold-brown, add 1% iron oxide and 1% manganese dioxide.

SPODUMENE MATT

Spar (C-6)	30
Dolomite	25
Ball Clay	25
Spodumene	20
Zircopax	15

This second glaze is a variation of the base glaze. It gives a rich cream to rust color with a nice waxy surface. No oxide additions are necessary.

Developing and Adjusting These Two Glazes: Our base glaze and our spodumene matt are variations of Rhodes 32 (see Appendix B, Glaze Recipes). The Rhodes glaze called for Oxford Spar, a potash spar which is less fluxing than a soda spar. For a slightly softer surface, not quite as dry a matt, we switched to C-6, a soda spar. We also added a small amount of nepheline syenite to flux the glaze even more. Rhodes' glaze recipe called for kaolin. We tend to use ball clay, because it helps keep the glaze materials in suspension better. (Ball clay has the potential to induce crawling, though. If this happens, you have got to go back to kaolin.)

If you need to substitute kinds of feldspar for some reason—you can't get one type, for example—most feldspars fall into two categories—potash and soda. Potash spars are less fluxing. If you substitute a potash for a soda spar in a glaze recipe, you will probably need to increase other fluxes somewhat—such as nepheline syenite and whiting (colemanite, talc, etc.) to compensate. (5–10% of these materials can lower the fusion temperature by as much as 50 °C.)

A Shiny Glaze:

WHITE LINER

Spar	41
Colemanite	12
Dolomite	7
Talc	15
Ball Clay	5
Flint	20

This liner glaze is referred to by both Dan Rhodes and Carlton Ball. It not only works well for lining casseroles, pitchers, teapots, etc., it is a good "bleeder" glaze.

Used under or over our matt glazes, it will bring out their color more clearly. For a more opacified satin white, 20% zircopax can be added.

An Ash Glaze: The standard proportions of 40 ash, 40 spar, and 20 clay make a nice ash glaze. This does vary with the type of wood you burn to get the ashes. If these proportions give a glaze surface that is too runny, add more clay; if the glaze is too stiff, add more spar or some whiting.

To mix up the glaze, take your fireplace ashes and run them through a 30-mesh screen. Mix the glaze materials with the ashes, add water, and run the mixture through a 30-mesh screen again. Wear rubber gloves—the mixture is very caustic.

Many studio potters in this country today are producing reduction-fired functional stoneware. They are firing in gas kilns which we have described in this chapter. The firing process described in the next chapter involves an entirely different method of reduction, a different firing cycle, and a much different end product.

CHAPTER **14**

Raku

We mentioned in the beginning of this book that we usually do a Raku firing with our students each year. Raku is a low-temperature firing technique involving a very rapid heating and cooling cycle. The pots are put into and removed from a red-hot kiln within a period of about fifteen minutes. If you are familiar with copper enameling, Raku is a very similar process.

Raku is a return to a more primitive treatment of clay. It has been made popular in western cultures by Bernard Leach, an English potter who spent a great deal of time in the East where Raku originated. Typical pieces are fairly thick, asymmetric in form, and handbuilt. The pots tend not to be very functional—they are both more porous and more fragile than traditionally fired stoneware. The natural forms of Raku are a refreshing contrast to the clean lines produced by wheel throwing and electric kiln glazing. See Fig. 14-1.

Raku is fun for students because it is usually done outside as a change of pace from the normal studio routine. Our Raku "parties" have usually taken place on one of the first warm weekends of spring and have been doubly enjoyable as a sort of "rites of spring" celebration (Fig. 14-2). Raku is exciting because students can follow their work from beginning to end and practically see it "come to life" right in front of them. The weather, the setting, the tempo, the flames and smoke, and the anticipation all combine to produce a dramatic spectacle.

PREPARATION

A couple of weeks before we intend to have our Raku firing, we give our students some special (grogged) clay to take home and make something with by hand. We stress

Fig. 14-1 Raku form; Regis C. Brodie. (*Courtesy of the artist*)

Fig. 14-2 Raku party.

159

that the pots will have to be handled by tongs when they are hot so must be pretty solid pieces. All construction must be joined well if slabs or coils are being combined. Fragile appendages should be avoided, and pots should be fairly heavy, natural, and direct.

Two of the ideas that worked particularly well this year were *beads* made of the Raku clay, glazed, and held on wires to fire. These were intended by their creators to become part of weavings or macrame hangings and were really effective. Pinched pots made with several *different clay colors* were also successful. The colored clays produced a much more subtle effect when covered with a clear glaze than the normal almost garish Raku glazes with strong oxides.

We have all the students bring their pots back a week before the Raku happening so we can dry and bisque-fire them all and have them ready to go. There is less breakage this way.

THE FIRING:
EQUIPMENT AND PROCEDURES

It is best to have everything ready to go beforehand. You will need the following:

• *A clay body.* We add 30% grog to our regular stoneware body. This is the easiest thing to do. Just wedge it in by hand.

• *Some base glazes.* We use the following two lead-free recipes: The first base consists of 75% colemanite (gerstley borate), 20% spar, and 5% Borax. The second contains 30% colemanite, 20% spar, 50% frit (P–311), and 2% bentonite as a suspending agent. These are clear glazes. You can add about 10% zircopax to either one for a white glaze.

• *Some oxides.* Cobalt, copper, and iron are good for a start. The oxides can be added to the base glaze directly. Make different batches for each color. 1% cobalt will give a distinct blue. 1–5% copper will yield a range between green in oxidation and red or metallic copper in reduction, usually both on the same pot. 1–5% iron will give tan to black.

These same oxides can be dissolved in water and worked with separately. Use one tablespoon of oxide per cup of water; but for cobalt, use only about a quarter as much. You can use these solutions in two ways. You can do decorative brushwork over or under the opacified white base glaze. Or, to produce the one-color effect of a regular glaze, you can sponge the solution over the entire pot. Then glaze it. This may also serve to highlight textures in the pot.

The sun may "adjust" the oxide concentration for you as the firing proceeds. You can also adjust them yourself after you see how the first fired pot comes out. After you have tried cobalt, copper, and iron, go to your shelf of oxides and begin experimenting with others.

We prefer this second method of keeping coloring oxides separate from the base glaze for several reasons. It does give beginning students a sense about glazes— how much is base and how little is coloring oxide. It is easier to adjust colors during firing and also easier to experiment with new colors. Plain base is always available for the pots which were pinched with colored clay and require no further decorating. Basically, this method gives us much more flexibility with a lot less preparatory work mixing glazes.

Whichever method you use, you should put the pots that you have finished glazing on top of the kiln to help dry the glazes thoroughly. This also serves to heat up the pots somewhat and decrease the risk of cracking when you place them in the kiln.

• *A kiln.* The kiln can be most anything. Uneven heat doesn't matter too much. One- to two-cubic-foot capacity is large enough. A 55-gallon drum with a Fiber-frax liner works fine. We use a small firebrick cube with a torch in one side. We put one kiln shelf inside (2″ off the floor) and use a second silicon carbide shelf as the roof. You can use this top kiln shelf as a "door," but you lose more heat this way. Our door consists of firebrick bolted into an angle iron frame which we pull back and forth in front (See Fig. 14-3). You can heat a Raku kiln to the necessary 950-1000°C with one burner and a 100-pound tank of propane, a very convenient method. It is also helpful to have a cement foundation of some sort under the kiln.

• *Raku tongs and asbestos gloves.* You definitely need these for handling the hot pots. Normally we run this part of the operation ourselves. Letting students handle the tongs to get pots in and out of the hot kiln involves too many potential hazards.

• *A pail of water and a pail of sawdust.* You will need a pail of water to plunge the smoking pot into at the end of the process to stop all reactions. You will also need a pail of sawdust or other organic material for "reducing" the pot. This second pail should have a cover.

This is how we do the reduction half of the process. After the pot has been in the kiln fifteen or twenty minutes and the glaze looks shiny and molten, we grasp it with the tongs, remove it from the kiln, and plunge it into the sawdust bucket (Fig. 14-4), immediately replacing the cover. After two or three minutes of reduction in

Fig. 14-3 Raku kiln showing side door, tongs, burner port in side, and pot drying and preheating on top.

Fig. 14-4 Reducing a Raku pot in bucket of woodchips (lid ready to put on).

the sawdust, we remove the lid, grasp the smoking pot with the tongs (it may burst into flames on contact with the air), and plunge the pot, carefully, into the bucket of water. After it cools for a while you can remove it, inspect it, and if you wish, scrub off the black residue with a Brillo pad or some sand.

This standard procedure can be varied in a number of ways to produce different results:

1. You can hold the pot (with the tongs) in the air for a minute before plunging it into the sawdust. This will cool it slightly and decrease the effect of reduction.

2. You can hold the pot in the air *after* the sawdust reduction and let it partially reoxidize before dousing it in water.

3. Instead of burying the pot in sawdust, you can hold the pot in the air and drop sawdust on one part of it only. It will burn and cause localized reduction, which will contrast with the rest of the oxidized surface of the pot.

4. Or you can use other organic materials. Grass clippings, hay, manure (which smells pretty bad), etc., can all be used to vary the type of reduction.

Although hard work is involved in the Raku firing, "playing" is really the order of the day. As new ideas and possibilities come up, follow them. Experiment. Safety is important, but you should not take your pots too seriously. The event is really more important than the end product.

CHAPTER 15

Constructing Your Own Slab Roller

George has designed a simple, inexpensive slab roller for studio use. It is made from easily available common materials and costs about $40.00. It is easy to construct if you have any kind of mechanical sense at all, and the finished slab roller works beautifully. It is designed to sit on a counter while you are working and can be put out of the way when you are finished.

LIST OF PARTS
FOR THE SLAB ROLLER

2 sets of appliance casters (Sears)
1 $^5/_8$ " (or $^3/_4$ ") sheet of plywood; 32 " × 48" for the *bottom board*
1 $^5/_8$ " (or $^3/_4$ ") sheet of plywood; 24" × 36" for the *top board*
4 cable clamps
4 eye bolts

2 angle iron pieces; 27 " long
2 bronze bushings
1 steel rod; 35 " × $^5/_8$ "
2 steel cables; 6 ' × $^1/_8$ "
1 2 " steel pipe; 27 " long, threaded
2 end-caps
24 sheet metal screws
1 steel bolt or steel nail
2 blocks of wood; 2 " × 4 " × 6 "
2 sheets of $^1/_8$ " thick masonite 24 " × 36 " (used to alter slab thickness)

ASSEMBLING THE SLAB ROLLER

Drawing of Guide Lines. With pencil, draw centerlines on the bottom board, separating it into four equal rectangles. Then, draw 4 " margins along the two long sides of the bottom board. You now have a bottom board divided into quarters with margins on either side.

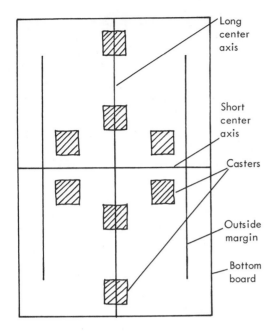

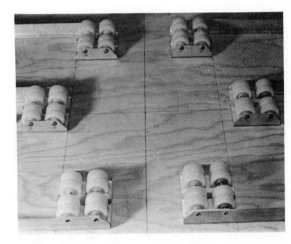

Fig. 15-1 Caster placement.

Placement of Casters. (See Fig. 15-1.) Set casters in place before attaching them. Set the first four casters 2″ from the outside margin-line in one direction and 2″ from the centerline in the other.

Set the next two casters on the long center axis, 6″ back from the short center axis. This will give stability to the top board when it is rolling.

Set the next two casters on the long center axis, 2″ from the outside edge of the bottom board.

Once you have set them in place, drill the bottom board and screw down the casters. Be very *careful* to get the casters exactly square, parallel and perpendicular to the edges of the bottom board and the center-lines.

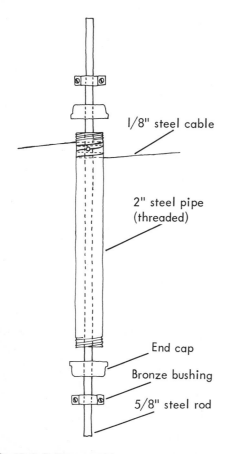

1/8" steel cable

2" steel pipe (threaded)

End cap

Bronze bushing

5/8" steel rod

Fig. 15-2 Roller assembly.

Assembling of Roller. (See Fig. 15-2.) Have your 2″ pipe cut and the ends threaded. Be sure the pipe surface doesn't get scored or deformed in the threading process. Screw on the end-caps; then have a ⅝″ hole drilled for you. The hole must be *exactly* on the center axis of the *pipe*. Do not drill the end-cap on center and assume that this will fall on the pipe's center axis. This is best done on a lathe. This is the most important step. It's worth paying someone else to do accurately. Otherwise, when you use the slab roller, you will get an up-and-down, washboard-like surface on your clay, and this uneven thickness is likely to cause warping.

Slide the ⅝″ steel rod through the roller; let 2″ extend from the opposite end-cap. You will have 2″ of rod on one end (to go through the bearing) and 4″ or more on the other end to go through the bearing and to have a handle (we use vice-grips) attached to it.

Drill a hole at either end of the pipe which passes through the center of the roller pipe and the center of the steel rod. This hole is for the steel bolt or nail that will keep the roller pipe and its center rod. connected to each other. They could be welded together if convenient, but the nail holds them fine.

Drill another set of holes for attaching the cables later on. These should be straight across from each other and ¾″ in from the edge of each end cap.

Attachment of the Roller Assembly to the Bottom Board. Set the 2″ × 4″ × 6″ blocks of wood on the outside edges of the bottom board at the centerline to support the roller assembly on either side, like a bridge.

Slide one bearing onto each end of the steel rod extending from the roller pipe.

Set the bearings on top of the 2″ × 4″ × 6″ blocks. Align so that the roller is *exactly* perpendicular to the long edges of the bottom board.

Adjust the distance between the bottom of the roller and the top of the rolling board. This distance will limit the maximum thickness of your rolled slab. We use a ¾″ rolling board, and our roller mounting is 2 ¾″ high, giving us ½″ maximum thickness for clay slabs. To make thinner slabs, one or more sheets of the ⅛″ masonite (Fig. 15-3) is then placed on top of the rolling board to increase its thickness and decrease the space the clay rolls through.

Fig. 15-3 ⅛″ masonite insert for rolling a thinner slab.

Attachment of Angle Iron Brace to Top Rolling Board. Drill two ¼″ holes in both angle iron braces, each one ¾″ in from either end. When the angle iron braces are attached to the top rolling board, these holes will be in the portion that extends beyond the edge of the board, for the purpose of attaching four screw eyes (see Fig. 15-4). Now drill several smaller holes in the angle iron, evenly spaced between the two larger holes, for the purpose of attaching the angle iron to the board.

Hold the angle iron braces on each end of the top rolling board. They should be flush with the bottom edge and extend 1½″ on either side. Use sheet metal screws through the small holes that you just drilled to attach the angle iron to the top rolling board. Then put the four screw eyes into the four larger holes on the ends of each brace.

You may need to "shim" the top side of the angle iron. If there is a space between the angle iron and the top of the plywood when the angle iron is flush with the bottom edge, fill in the space with a narrow strip of wood.

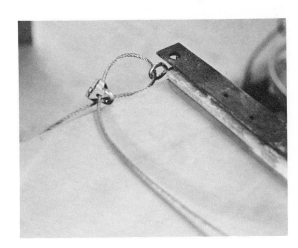

Fig. 15-4 Top rolling board with cable attached to angle iron.

Mounting and Adjustment of the Cable.
Stand in front of your partially constructed
slab roller with the steel pipe roller assembly perpendicular to you. Roll the top
board under the pipe (and over the casters)
pushing it almost as far to your right as you
can. The left-hand end of the top board
should stop two inches from the center
roller.

Fold one of the cables in half to determine its center point (do not crease). Open
up the cable at this point, and slide a sheet
metal screw through the middle—an equal
number of metal strands on either side of
the screw (Fig. 15-5). Repeat with second
cable. Screw the midpoint of each cable to
the roller. (Holes were left there in an
earlier step.)

You now have the roller with the cables
resting on top of it—the screw attaching
cables to roller on top. The top rolling

Fig. 15-5 Attaching the cable to the roller.

board has been slid to the right so that its
left edge is 2″ from the roller.

Take the left-hand end of the cable
nearest you and feed it under the roller and
out the other side. Pull it through all the
way to the right side, and put it through the
screw eye on the right end of the top rolling
board. Clamp loosely. Repeat on the
other side—still working from the short
side of the rolling board, under the roller,
and out to the long side of the board. Both
screw eyes on the same end (originally the
right end as you faced your slab roller) will
now have cables attached to them.

Now take the right end of the cable and
feed it under the roller from right to left.
Repeat twice more, making three clock-wise
cable rotations around the roller. Then
extend the remaining length of cable to the
left, just a few inches, through the screw
eye on the left end of the top rolling board,
and clamp loosely. Go around to the other
side of the slab roller and repeat the
procedure.

Attach a vice-grip, as a handle, to the
rod extending from the steel roller. Carefully roll the center rod, which will drive
the top board now that the cables are
attached. Rotate clockwise as far as it will
go to see that the cables are long enough to
allow you full use of the total length of the
top board. After you have checked this in
both directions, clamp the cable clamps
down tightly. Finer adjustments in tight-
ness of the cable can be made at any time
by screwing the screw eyes in or out a few
rotations. The final adjustment is made by
tightening the screw eye bolts so that the
top board runs true.

CHAPTER **16**

Plaster

If you are throwing on a wheel, you may need to know how to make your own plaster bats. For wedging clay, you will find a plaster wedging table useful. If you are handbuilding with slabs, plaster drape molds or press molds may be necessary. Very often, working with clay leads to working with plaster as well. It is not difficult if you follow the procedures described in the following pages.

PREPARATION

The Plaster. The first thing you will need is a bag of dry plaster. Buy either pottery plaster from a ceramic supplier or pure plaster of Paris. Do *not* use construction plaster; it has too many contaminants in it. Try to use your plaster within two or three months of buying it. Store it temporarily in a plastic bag, and put this in a covered garbage can. Plaster tends to absorb moisture from the air, and if this happens, it will not react properly when you mix and pour it.

The Mold. Molds may be bought, found around the house, or constructed. Aluminum pie tins make good bat molds. Or buy commercially made ones if fit is important. To make a wedging table, construct a square frame by attaching four boards to each other. Seal the corners tightly. For drape molds, plastic bowls will often work. The shape of the mold is important. A slight outward taper insures that the mold will release from the hardened plaster. If you have a reverse taper, the mold will not release.

Occasionally the surface of your counter becomes part of your mold, so find a smooth, flat, and *level* surface to work on. A formica counter is excellent.

To prepare your mold for the poured plaster, you will need to "size" it. Sizing serves the same purpose as greasing a bread-pan before filling it for baking. In fact, salad oil is a good sizing material. Or you can buy special mold soap (Fig. 16-1).

If the mold must be sealed to the counter top, this latter also must be sized. Commercially made bat molds or a frame for a wedging the table are two common types of molds which use the counter top as one side and must therefore be sealed down. Use a coil of clay around the outside of the mold to seal it securely so no plaster can leak out. Sometimes weights are useful, in addition, to hold the form down tight. If you are using containers such as pie tins or bowls for molds, these will be used right side up and require no sealing.

Tools and Utensils. It is important to have the mold ready and all accessories together in one place before you add the plaster to the water. Once you do this, a reaction begins which cannot be stopped or slowed down to allow you to run around looking for something you forgot. You may even want to make yourself a checklist and consult it beforehand.

Some tools and utensils to have ready are a scale, a screen, and a striker. You need the scale for weighing out the plaster and the water. A bathroom scale will work. You need the screen for breaking up lumps in the plaster. The screen you use for mixing glazes is fine. A window screen will also work. For a striker, you can use a short, straight board, a ruler, or a hacksaw blade. This is for smoothing off the surface of the hardening plaster.

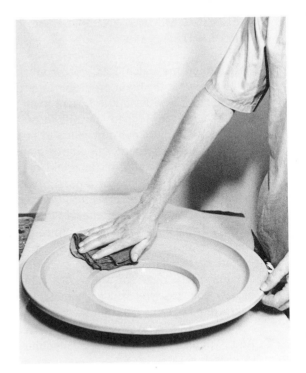

Fig. 16-1 Soaping the mold.

You should have on hand a disposable container for whatever plaster-mix is left over after you fill the mold.

You will also need three pails. Size one of the pails with mold soap or oil, and use this pail for the measured water. This is the pail you will pour the plaster-mix from, and you will need to clean it immediately after pouring. The sizing will ease the clean-up chore. The second pail is for the weighed-out and screened dry plaster. As you proceed, you will pour the dry plaster out of this pail and into the first pail. The third pail should contain warm water for clean-up. Hands, containers, and tools cannot be washed in the sink. Plaster continues to set up and will clog the drain. If you prefer, you can use an outside hose for clean-up if it is readily accessible.

WEIGHING, MIXING, AND POURING THE PLASTER

Determining the Batch Size. "How much will I need?" is the main problem you will have to grapple with. You will want to mix up only a little more than you will need at one time. To figure out how much to mix up, you must determine the approximate volume of your mold. If the mold is a container such as a bowl or a pie tin, you can fill it with water and measure its volume directly. (A quart of water equals 57 cubic inches.) Otherwise, you will have to calculate the volume.

Here are two important rules:
- For every quart of water (57 cubic inches) you use, you will get almost 1⅓ quarts of plaster mix (80 cubic inches).
- Use a 10:6 ratio of plaster to water. Add 10 pounds of plaster to every 6 pounds (3 quarts) of water.

You will understand this more clearly from the following example. Let's suppose that you have a mold that holds almost a full gallon (4 quarts) of water. If, as stated above, every quart of water yields almost 1⅓ quarts of mix, you can readily see that 3 quarts of water will yield almost 4 quarts of mix, or the desired amount in this case. Remembering the old adage a pint's a pound the world around, you know that a quart weighs 2 pounds and therefore that 3 quarts weighs 6 pounds. If you have 6 pounds of water in your mix, then, the second rule mentioned above tells you that you will need to add 10 pounds of plaster to it. So, a batch containing 6 pounds of water and 10 pounds of plaster will fill a mold that is just under 4 quarts in volume. By following our two rules, you should be able to adjust for smaller or larger batch sizes.

Weighing Out and Mixing the Plaster and Water. The water temperature should be between 60° and 65°F. Water temperature affects the rate at which the plaster-mix sets up. Measure out the required amount of water. In the case of our example above, you would weigh or measure 3 quarts or 6 pounds. Pour this into a sized (greased) pail to help later on in clean-up.

Weigh out your plaster, 10 pounds in this case. Screen it into the second pail to break up any lumps.

Make sure that everything is ready before you proceed.

To mix, *add the plaster to the water.* Let it sit for about 2 minutes. *Do not* stir immediately. Then hand-mix preferably with your fingers (Fig. 16–2). Do not use a beater. If your water was at 60°F, you will need to stir for 5 or 6 minutes before the plaster begins to thicken. When you can draw a line across the top of the plaster that remains visible, the plaster is ready to pour (Fig. 16–3). Do not wait until you can form peaks in the plaster with your finger; this is too late.

Pouring the Plaster. When you think the plaster-mix is ready, pour it immediately into the mold (Fig. 16–4). You have only about 1 minute leeway. Pour the excess plaster immediately into a box or container for that purpose, and clean out the plaster bucket. Use either an outside hose or your third pail of warm water for clean-up, *not* the sink. If your plaster started to pile up as you poured it, you waited a little too long. If water comes to the surface, you poured too soon. If you erred only slightly in one direction or the other, you will probably still end up with a usable plaster form (Fig. 16–5).

Fig. 16-2 Mixing the plaster.

Fig. 16-3 Testing plaster to see if it's ready to pour.

Fig. 16-4 Pouring plaster into mold.

Fig. 16-5 Just in time.

Finishing. Five minutes or so after you have poured your mold, the plaster will begin to heat up. This is the time to smooth off the top of the mold. A hacksaw blade or anything straight will work as a striker. Remove all excess plaster smoothly, by scraping the blade across the top.

The easiest time to remove the form from the mold is after the plaster has finished heating, just as it begins to cool. It will still be very soft but firm. You can wait longer if necessary. Light taps on the mold should release the plaster.

Sharp corners or uneven edges should be smoothed or beveled. Surform, a tool recommended earlier for trimming pots, works beautifully for trimming plaster. This is best done within a day of pouring—before the plaster is totally dry.

Let plaster bats dry 1 or 2 weeks before you use them. To "break in" the bat, string your first pot. Do not rely on the plaster to release it. When you clean off the bat afterward, you will remove the thin film of dry plaster on it, and it will be ready to use after that. You will need to use this "breaking-in" process before you use molds as well.

CHAPTER **17**

Photographing Pots

The most common reason for wanting to take good photographs of pots is to send them to juries when applying for shows. Generally, colored slides are required. If an occasional show is your only need for slides, or if you know a professional photographer who will trade pots for photographing sessions, your best bet may be to let someone else do it. However, many potters find it increasingly desirable to have the equipment and skills necessary for taking adequate pictures of their own work on a regular basis. In addition to color slides, black and white glossies are often in demand for newspaper publicity. The instructions on equipment, background, lighting, and composition in this chapter will apply for both color and black and white photography.

This chapter was written with the help of Rob Howard, crafts photographer.

EQUIPMENT

A camera. Any camera that uses 35 mm film is sufficient.

A light meter. This may be built into the camera or be separate.

A gray card. These are available for a dollar at photographic supply stores. They show you what the light meter sees and are very helpful for an amateur photographer. Clear instructions accompany the card.

A tripod.

Two photo-flood lights with bowl reflectors.

A reflector, an absorber, and a diffuser of light. These can be homemade. A sheet of aluminum foil with a "door" cut in it can be used to cover the photo-flood and direct the light in a specific direction. A piece of matt board can be converted into both a reflector and an absorber of light. Cover one side with crinkled aluminum foil to serve as a reflector; cover the other with black velvet to act as an absorber. You will almost certainly need something to diffuse the light as well. A piece of frosted plexiglass works perfectly for this.

Film. For color slides, we recommend High-speed Ektachrome, Type B (indoor) film ASA 125. For black and white, we use Kodak Plus-X, ASA 125, the same film speed as Highspeed Ektachrome. This eliminates a variable when switching back and forth between color and black and white photography.

A notebook to record your first few sessions so when the slides or photos come back from the processor, you will know what worked and what didn't.

If you are going to achieve some measure of success in photographing your own work, and you can, you should standardize the equipment and procedures you use as much as possible. Use the same lights, the same film type, and the same background to begin with.

BACKGROUND

In selecting a background, consider both tone and texture. In tone, the background should contrast with the pot so that one is clearly separated from the other (see Figs. 17-1 and 17-2). The background can have a certain amount of texture as long as it is

Fig. 17-1 Black vase; Edwin and Mary Scheier. White linear sgraffito decoration, white background. (*Courtesy League of New Hampshire Craftsmen*)

Fig. 17-2 White porcelain dragon mirror; Pat Probst Gilman. Black velvet background. (*Courtesy of the artist*) (*Photo by Ruth Pasquine*)

Fig. 17-3 Tea set; George & Nancy Wettlaufer. Illustrates a natural background that is much too competitive.

priate to the earthiness of the medium. And although there are more variables to deal with outside, you may, with experience, be able to obtain truer colors from the natural light. Be careful to find a background that is not too busy and doesn't swallow up or compete with your pot (see Figs. 17–3 and 17–4).

LIGHTING

Photographing with One Light. Using one light is easy, and it can be very effective. We are all used to the concept of only one sun. To keep your first session simple, you may want to use the same pot so you will understand more clearly how the different positions of the light affect the character of the photographed pot. The first position to set your light in is very near the camera, up a little higher than the camera so that it shines straight at the pot and down at about a 45° angle. (See Fig. 17–5). Lighting of this sort is very even, somewhat on the

subordinate and noncompetitive with the pot being photographed. For both color and black and white photographs, a neutral background, black, gray, or off-white, is effective and versatile. A colored background may distort the colors in the pot if you are doing color photography. Try unbleached muslin if your pots are in the mid- to dark-tone range. Avoid a satin fabric or any shiny surface which could give highlights or reflections.

Either fabric or seamless paper works well as a background, because they can be draped in a smooth curve to eliminate a horizon line behind the pot. If you use fabric, make sure it is free of wrinkles. For a smooth, nonreflective background, a piece of illustration board will work well. If your pots are large, you may need seamless paper, which you can get at a photographic supply store. Find one background that works well, and stick with it to begin with.

Later on you may want to experiment with outdoor photography in natural settings. Many potters feel that this is appro-

Fig. 17-4 Bowls; Val Cushing. The smooth satin surface of the bowls contrasts with the rough textured boards producing a successful natural-setting photograph.

bland side. Since very little shadow is produced, neither shape nor texture is accentuated. However, it is useful because of its simplicity.

Now move your one light to the side so that it is at 45° to the pot–camera axis. (See Fig. 17–6). This second lighting set-up will introduce a shadow that falls on the side of the pot opposite the light. The suggestion of three dimensions in photography depends on the positioning of highlights and shadows. By having a shadow on part of the pot and varying degrees of light on other parts, a sense of form and dimension is more apparent. Normally, the camera elevation is slightly higher than the center of the pot. This also contributes to three-dimensionality by enabling you to see the inside of the opposite rim of the pot, part of the lid, etc. You may want to experiment with various heights for your camera in this respect as well. Try to perfect this particular lighting set-up; it's a good workhorse.

Continue to move your single light source until it is at 90° to the pot–camera axis. (See Fig. 17–7). This third lighting set-up is often called "dramatic" lighting, since the pot is divided into light and dark down the middle. A coarse texture becomes most apparent with this type of lighting. The raised areas of the surface catch the light, while the receding areas remain in the shade. In many instances, this third type of lighting is not the best for a jury slide, since so much of the pot is shaded. Normally, you want to convey as much information about your work as possible. However, since you can never show everything in a photo, this will involve an element of compromise.

If you are relatively new to photography, try these three lighting set-ups without

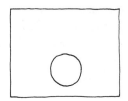

Fig. 17-5 Light parallel to the camera-subject axis.

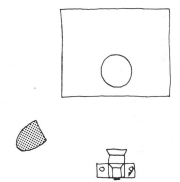

Fig. 17-6 Light at 45° to the camera-subject axis.

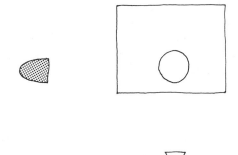

Fig. 17-7 Light at 90° to the camera-subject axis.

actually shooting the photos. View the pot carefully through the viewfinder of the camera after you change the angle of the light or of the camera. What you see in the viewfinder is very close to what your photo will be.

Examples of Pots Photographed with One Light. The following black and white photographs were taken in a corner of our studio by Rob Howard with a Canon FTb, using Kodak Plus-X film, ASA 125, and a 100 mm lens. They are called "table top still lifes." If you have a little extra room in your studio, set up a permanent place for photographing sessions so you'll do it more often.

The first pot we photographed was a wine jug by Pat Probst Gilman. We felt that the texture was the most important aspect of the pot, so we used the "dramatic" lighting set-up with the light at right-angles to the pot (see Figs. 17–8 and 17–9). The pitcher by Carl Sande, by contrast, has a very smooth shiny surface. In the first photo of the pitcher, we repeated the dramatic lighting set-up we had used with the rough-textured wine jug (see Figs. 17–10 and 17–11). The second photo of the pitcher was taken with the light at 45° to the pot–camera axis (see Figs. 17–12 and 17–13). You can see the two very different effects achieved simply by changing the angle at which the pot was lighted.

Fig. 17–8 Wine jug; Pat Probst Gilman, 1966.

Fig. 17–9 Diagram of "dramatic" lighting set-up used for Fig. 17–8.

Fig. 17-10 Stoneware pitcher; Carl Sande, 1974. Saturated iron glaze.

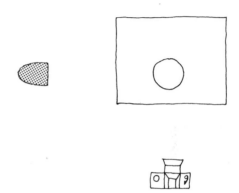

Fig. 17-11 Diagram of lighting set-up for Fig. 17-10; light at 90° to the camera–subject axis.

Fig. 17-12 Same pitcher photographed with different lighting set-up.

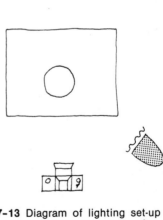

Fig. 17-13 Diagram of lighting set-up for Fig. 17-12; diffused light (causing softer shadow than in Fig. 17-10) at 45° to the camera–subject axis.

Photographing with Two Lights. When you use two lights, one becomes the "main" light and the other is used as "fill." There is an alternative to the two-light set-up if you have a reflector, such as the matt board covered with aluminum foil. You may want to try this as your "fill" with a single light source before proceeding to two lights. In working with two lights, be careful to avoid double shadows whenever possible.

Certain problems involved in the two-light set-up, such as double shadows, extra highlights, the lighting ratio (which we haven't explained here), can be eliminated if you diffuse both lights. The Wettlaufer sphere (see Figs. 17-14 and 17-15) was taken with two lights, both at 45° and both diffused. This is generally called "museum" lighting, a technique which produces a lot of light on the object and eliminates unwanted and distracting reflections as well as most shadows. If you are going to photograph pots with shiny glazes, this may be the best lighting set-up. You may even want to construct an opaque light tent, a cubical frame covered with material such as tissue paper, sheer fabric, or plexiglass. Set the pot to be photographed inside this, and all light reaching it will be diffused. For more information on light tents, read *Photography for Artists and Craftsmen* by Claus-Peter Schmid, an excellent reference on all aspects of photographing crafts.

COMPOSITION

So far, we have talked about the two major factors you will need to learn to control in taking good photographs of your pots—background and lighting. A third concept is also important, that of arrangement or composition. Here are some things to consider.

Try to fill the whole frame, especially in the case of colored slides for juries.

Off-set the pot slightly to left or right of center to avoid a static "bulls-eye" effect.

In the case of something like a pitcher or a teapot, when you want to show both lip or spout as well as the handle opposite it, rotate the pot slightly *more than* 90° away

Fig. 17-14 Sphere; George & Nancy Wettlaufer, 1974.

Fig. 17-15 Diagram of "museum" lighting set-up for Fig. 17-14; two lights (both diffused) at 45° to the camera–subject axis.

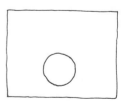

Fig. 17-16 Stoneware tea set; Ruth McKinley, Canada, 1975. Wood-fired, cone 9-10 reduction. *(Courtesy of the artist) (Photo by Donald L. McKinley)*

from the camera axis to avoid a static effect.

If there is an important detail that you want to show, make sure it is in the lighted area of the pot.

Camera Angle. Normally, the camera is positioned slightly higher than the center of the pot. Occasionally, you may need to raise the camera to show decorative details that are important, such as on the lid of a casserole, for example. Try not to get so high that you distort the profile of the pot, however. This is a compromise situation.

Look through the viewfinder again. Have you eliminated table edges, horizon lines, or other background clutter that will be distracting?

Arrangement is important in photographing sets or groups of objects. Experiment with different ways of positioning the pots. See Fig. 17-16. Ruth McKinley's beautiful tea set has been superbly arranged and photographed by her husband Donald McKinley.

Photographing your pots forces you to take time to evaluate your work through the cold eye of the camera. You will gain valuable insights from these sessions.

"During this process of intense visualization, you may experience the excitement of rediscovering your art through the medium of photography."*

*From Photography for Artists and Craftsmen

CHAPTER **18**

Selling
Your
Work

If you work with clay regularly and have a permanent studio set-up, you may eventually want to sell some of your work. This might be to help pay for materials and continue your hobby, or it might eventually lead to a substantial income, even a living. We have been supporting a family of four as potters for the last four years. Much of what we learned about selling was trial and error. It prompted us to write our first book, *The Craftsman's Survival Manual,* to share these experiences with others. We have found that the following general rules, distilled from *The Craftsman's Survival Manual,* work very well for us. The rules may also be helpful to you if you are thinking about or already getting started selling your pots.

DON'T START SELLING TOO SOON

You should be glazing and firing yourself, have adequate production facilities, and have a distinctive style to your work. You are *not* ready to sell your work after eight lessons. A bad reputation is difficult to overcome even if your work improves.

Remember, when you are making pots for a hobby, the "success" of a pot is measured subjectively. Did you enjoy making the pot? Once you begin selling, a pot must be successful in aesthetic and technical terms, regardless of how therapeutic an experience making it might have been. Be harsh on yourself in judging your work. Otherwise, it may come back to haunt you.

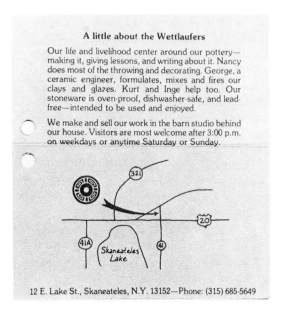

A little about the Wettlaufers

Our life and livelihood center around our pottery—making it, giving lessons, and writing about it. Nancy does most of the throwing and decorating. George, a ceramic engineer, formulates, mixes and fires our clays and glazes. Kurt and Inge help too. Our stoneware is oven-proof, dishwasher-safe, and lead-free—intended to be used and enjoyed.

We make and sell our work in the barn studio behind our house. Visitors are most welcome after 3:00 p.m. on weekdays or anytime Saturday or Sunday.

12 E. Lake St., Skaneateles, N.Y. 13152—Phone: (315) 685-5649

Fig. 18-1 Inside of tag we attach to all our pots.

george and nancy wettlaufer

Authors of
The Craftsman's Survival Manual
and Getting Into Pots

Fig. 18-2 Outside of tag we attach to all of our pots.

Fig. 18-3 Silk-screening logo on bags.

BE PROFESSIONAL

Present a quality image of yourself. Display your work well.

Attach to your pots a *tag* which contains a logo or photo, consumer information, such as "oven proof, lead-free," etc., and your name and address (Figs. 18–1 and 18–2). A letterhead with the same logo (even bags) also gives customers the impression that you are stable and business-like (Fig. 18–3).

Be reliable. Stand behind your work, don't take orders you can't fill, and continue to maintain the same or better-quality standards. Develop and grow personally.

Be willing to take time to educate others about your work—the general public, shop

owners, other craftsmen, etc. Talk to people, let them tour your studio, and make them aware of what constitutes "quality" in your opinion. Take clay to the local Brownie troops or nursery school for a day if they invite you. Consider taking on an apprentice (but do some reading and talking about this first to make sure you can handle it).

PREFER RETAIL SELLING—
DO NOT WHOLESALE
YOUR TOTAL INVENTORY

Few craftsmen can afford to give a 50% discount on all their work and still stay in business. Although retail selling takes time and money, you can still come out ahead. Wholesaling to shops seems to work best to fill in slow times of the year. We prefer to sell our own work, at retail prices, whenever possible.

If you are located near civilization, encourage people to come and buy pots at your studio. This will begin to happen

Fig. 18-4 Dinner set by the Wettlaufers.

naturally if all your pots have a tag tied on them which includes your address. Also, *keep a list* of good customers who buy from you at fairs or out of the studio. Have an *open house* once or twice a year, and mail invitations to those on your list. This *really* pays off and may also lead to large custom orders such as the dinner set pictures in Fig. 18-4.

Ferret out and attend a few worthwhile (high quality–high sales) retail craft fairs, where it's worth your time and energy to set up and sell your own work for a few days. This is a good change of pace and usually a good time, and if the entry fee is low and sales high, you can come home in good shape financially.

IF SELLING TO SHOPS,
PREFER OUTRIGHT SELLING
TO CONSIGNMENT

Visit the shops you sell to first. Make sure of the quality level and appropriateness of the shop. Do you like the owner?

If you attend a wholesale show, you may be approached by shopowners you do not know. Before accepting an order from them, you may want to ask for references of three craftsmen they have done business with and then check with the other craftsmen. Ask the shopowner if he has a picture of his shop to show you as well.

Be careful not to saturate an area. There is an advantage to selling fairly locally so you can avoid shipping, which is a nuisance, but it's not fair to shops to sell to others in the same area.

Encourage flexible orders—two dozen pots in a range of colors and prices—and encourage balanced orders—don't let a shopowner order everything under $5.00 or only one style of pot. People seeing your work in that shop may think that that's all you know how to do.

PRICE REASONABLY

Try not to over- or under-price your work. Compare your work to others; see what their prices are. Figure out your time and material costs. If you are going to err, be *slightly* on the low side at first. It's better to sell your work and have it out in homes —forcing you to keep moving forward— than to have it sitting in your studio while you remain unknown, get discouraged, and go into debt. Adjust upward if prices go up (materials and overhead), if your quality improves; or if your work is selling too fast.

If you're making pots part-time, try not to undercut people making pots for a living.

Decide whether you're making art or pots. People who think they're doing art tend to price higher. If the work is really unique or exceptional, this may be justifiable.

DON'T LET YOURSELF BE OVERLY AFFECTED BY A JURY'S JUDGMENT

In general, a jury statement says more about them than it does about you, regardless of whether you were accepted or rejected. Try to evaluate realistically whatever comments are sent back to you.

Rejection or acceptance into a juried show may be based more on the quality of your slides than that of your pots. Learn to photograph your work well.

What juries are looking for is often not what the buying public is interested in.

Ironically, rejection from a juried show sometimes means that your work is "commercial," what the buying public is after, but not unique enough in the eyes of an art-oriented jury.

DEVELOP SOME RHYTHMS

Production rhythms in the studio and seasonal rhythms for selling are both important. Figure out what your peak seasons are, how much you can make, how many shows spaced how far apart you can reasonably attend, how much wholesaling you can handle, etc. Then plan accordingly so you can avoid last minute frenzy. In general, it is better to use the slow times for filling orders, developing new techniques and designs, etc. Summer and Christmas tend to be peak times here. Sales are slower in February and then pick up before Easter. By taking a vacation in February, we don't miss much and also avoid the high fuel bills resulting from heating the barn-studio.

Order supplies way ahead so you don't run out at peak times. If shortages of particular materials are a problem, be especially careful not to get too low.

KEEP RECORDS

If you don't know how to set up a bookkeeping system, have an accountant help you. Keep track of how much you make and how much you spend. If you keep a checkbook for expenses and sales pads for sales, most of your transactions are automatically recorded for you. Sales tax, in those states requiring it, *must* be collected on each retail sale and paid to the state quarterly; *do it.*

THINK SMALL—KEEP YOUR OVERHEAD DOWN

Keep your business small and personal. Don't go into partnership. Don't succumb to the pressures to grow. You risk giving up your freedom and your way of life in return for a lot of hassles and, often, not much increase in income. The quality of your work may tend to suffer as well.

Remember, crafts are popular because of their personal nature. Customers need an alternative to G.E., Standard Oil, and Sears Roebuck. They like to know that something was made carefully by an individual who cared about his work, not cranked out mindlessly by a machine. And your simple way of life is what the average 9-5 commuter is buying as much as your carefully made pot. Keep your freedom—it's more important than a few extra dollars.

CHAPTER **19**

Teaching Pottery in School

Neither of us is an art teacher although George taught industrial arts for a while and Nancy taught French and German. We have friends and relatives teaching art. In general, we are fairly aware of the school situation. Here are some of the things we think we'd try to do with ceramics classes if we were teaching them in the public schools. (In some schools, the budget and procedure for ordering materials and equipment are very restrictive—especially where art teachers are required to order through a purchasing agent who sends out for bids. If at all possible, we would want to be in charge of ordering our own supplies—within the allotted budget.)

OBJECTIVES IN THE ART CLASSROOM

We would be inclined to work more with textures and colored clays and engobes for decoration; less with glazes—assuming electric kiln firing. (See Section II on glazing and firing.)

In teaching the wheel, we would try to use a method (the instructional method of Section I) rather than sending students off to the corner alone to play on the one or two wheels there. When we teach wheel throwing in our studio, we try to give a lot of positive reinforcement to our students—let them feel *right* feelings first before

Fig. 19-1 First grade students working with clay.

experimenting with wrong feelings. We also try to limit frustration by offering help when needed. Not only does this produce less discouragement, which working on the wheel certainly can produce, it will give the students a pot to carry through the rest of the way—to learn trimming, texturing, glazing, etc.

In the balance required between freedom to experiment and discipline to master skills, we would be more inclined to let freedom reign with the handbuilding and require an attempt at mastery over wheel-throwing skills (within reason).

We would try to involve the students in mixing up glazes, stacking kilns, firing pots etc., so they would become more realistic about the total process. This would take some organizing and rotation, with only a few students involved at a time.

We would try to do a different type of firing, such as Raku (see Chapter 14) for a change of pace. This also involves the students very directly with the total process and teaches "reduction," which they will be unaware of if you are firing electric.

In a section called "schools and raku," Finn Lynggaard expresses some of our own concerns in his book *Pottery: Raku Technique:*

Many schools nowadays are well equipped with pottery rooms and expensive equipment. Even so, it is particularly distressing to a professional potter to see the lack of understanding and ill-informed attitude towards elementary ceramic processes that can result, for example, in the pupils being allowed to shape their own pieces of pottery which are afterwards fired by the teacher and the pupils finally painting the fired articles with gay poster paints. . . . The raku technique can give children a first-hand knowledge of the whole ceramic miracle, and the process will come home to them in a far more vivid way when they themselves can take part in it from A to Z. They will be thrilled by the quick results, in contrast to the usual system which has a great disadvantage that the time between the moment when the things are made until they are finished is very long.

We would try to relate pottery to as many other subjects in school and in the outside world as possible.

RELATING CLAY TO THE NATURAL WORLD

One good way to do this is to find a clay outcrop near the school and take the students (if it can be arranged) to dig some clay. This is more realistic than pulling it out of plastic bags.

Point out the difference between clay—inorganic, formed from rocks eroding and weathering—and garden soil—mostly organic, formed from plant and animal matter decaying. It is usually possible on a walk of this kind to find examples of quartz (silica), hematite (natural iron oxide), and other minerals present in clays or glazes. Is there anything you could take back and grind up and try in your clay body for speckles?

If you dig clay up and bring it back to the studio, you will need to find out two things about it—its plasticity and its maturing temperature. For purposes of experimenting, pinch a small pot, let it dry, and fire it to the temperature you normally fire to. Set it on top of a small bisqued plate. You may be surprised to discover that it looks more like a glaze than a clay when you take it out of the kiln. Albany slip is such a natural material. Your first decision, then, will be whether to use this natural substance as a clay or as a glaze.

If it looks more like a glaze than a clay but still has a dry matt surface, try adding more flux. Colemanite or nepheline syenite in graduated amounts will improve the surface.

If you decide that this material is more clay-like, you may need to adjust both its plasticity and its maturing temperature. Put some water in your fired pinch pot. Is the pot very porous or very dense? If it is very dense, add some fire clay to raise the maturing temperature. If it is very porous, add some feldspar to lower the maturing temperature.

You may also need to adjust its plasticity. If the clay is too plastic, it will feel sticky, have a high amount of shrinkage, and tend to crack in drying and firing. Add grog or fire clay; their coarser particles will counteract this. If it is not plastic enough, especially if you wish to throw on the wheel with it, add some ball clay (fine-particled clay). Finding natural clays and adjusting them to suit your purposes is a great learning experience.

Further awareness of natural resources might come from talking about industrial users of clay—the traditional ones as well as those that students might be unaware of. Do they know that paper companies are one of the largest users of clay? (They need it for the shiny coating on magazine pages.) Do they realize that clay contains alumina, which may shortly be used by aluminum can companies—if they can figure out an economic way of extracting it—now that bauxite is running out? If the paper and can industries, as well as the ceramic industries, consume tons of clay a year, how long will it last? (Doesn't it make more sense to use returnable glass bottles for beer and soft drinks instead of disposable aluminum cans?) It's important to talk about clay in terms of natural resources—and their diminishing supply.

At the same time, we would tend to be frugal with clay in the classroom, reclaiming whenever possible. This is easily done. Let scraps of clay and unwanted pots dry out completely, break them up into small pieces, throw them into a garbage can, and add water, or slop from throwing, to the can. After it has soaked a couple of days, drain off the excess water, spread the clay out on bats (or run it through a pug-mill) and rewedge it. Clay can be reused indefinitely this way. If we were teaching ceramics in a classroom, we would want a pug mill as the next investment after a kiln and a few wheels.

RELATING DESIGN TO NATURE

Since clay is a natural material, it is best treated as such aesthetically as well as technically at the beginning. On the field trip you take to dig clay, for example, students might take a notebook along and make notations of shapes, textures, and other ideas from nature that come into their heads. Collect some leaves or grasses or shells to bring back for inspiration or for direct textural use.

We do not recommend, especially for beginners, designing pots on paper first and then trying to throw them. Very contrived, often overworked, and unspontaneous pots tend to result. But, on the other hand, it is helpful to keep some of your notebook ideas from nature in mind so you can try to incorporate them when feasible. See Fig. 19–2.

Fig. 19-2 Earth form; Isabel Parks, Warren Hullow. (*From the authors' collection*)

RELATING POTS TO HISTORY, CULTURE, AND ANTHROPOLOGY

Have students bring in pots from their families' collections that represent other than 20th century American craftsmanship. Or bring some in yourself—real ones or slides of them. Or, go to a museum exhibit. Invite a history or anthropology teacher to the class to talk about the civilizations that produced these pots. Pottery is a good core subject from which to branch into history, because almost all civilizations from all ages have made functional pots for daily use. How did they do it? What materials and equipment did they have? What temperatures could they fire to, and what did they use for fuel, etc.? What forms did they make and for what purpose?

RELATING POTTERY TO 20th CENTURY LIFE-STYLES

Take the class to a nearby craft fair, if at all possible. Talk to different potters about their work and their lives. As you go from one booth to another, ask yourselves the following questions:

• How were the various types of pots fired—oxidation or reduction? low or high temperatures? salt-glazed, wood-fired, or other?

• How were they formed—thrown or built? How were they decorated—at leather-hard? after bisque-firing? other?

• How is the craftsmanship? Are the thrown pots well trimmed, handles well attached, etc.? Are handbuilt pots well constructed, no seams coming apart? Was the glaze applied well? Did it run down on the bottoms and need to be ground off? Do you find warping or cracking?

• Write down ideas in your notebook—don't copy anything, but take note of some things you think you might like to try when you are back working with clay yourself.

• Talk about how the work is displayed. What types of pottery are selling best? What personal reactions—positive or negative—do you have to the craft fair in general? How many of the craftsmen there are making their living at pottery?

Another way to relate pottery to present day life-styles is to visit a potter in his studio—if he's willing. How does this set-up differ from the classroom set-up? Or have a studio potter come in and demonstrate and talk about his work and his life as a craftsman.

Another very interesting field-trip, for contrast, might be to a factory that makes things from clay industrially—a factory that makes dinnerware or one that manufactures sinks, toilets, tiles, etc. What does industry do that a studio potter does not? What similarities can you find?

Fig. 19-3 Abraxas; Jeffrey Pacek.

Fig. 19-4 Figurative family; Elly Mout.

Fig. 19-5 Tree trunk; Ricky Mondolo.

ENTER A STUDENT EXHIBIT OR PUT ON YOUR OWN EXHIBIT

Competitiveness is not the goal here, but awareness of exhibiting pottery well—what backgrounds are most appropriate for example? Learn to display your work well; have those who are interested in photography work on lighting and photographing the exhibit. See Figs. 19-3, 19-4, and 19-5, high school students' pots exhibited at the Carborundum Museum of Ceramics in 1975.

RELATE CLAY TO OTHER MEDIA

Photography was just mentioned. Photographic silk-screening combined with pottery as a decorative technique is receiving a lot of attention lately. For students interested in both photography and pottery, this might be an interesting challenge.

Clay can be related to any number of art media. Several people have spoken to us recently about doing porcelain faces for soft-sculpture human figures they are working on. Clay can be combined with weaving and macrame by means of beads and irregular pieces which can be incorporated into the piece—or clay pieces (with holes in them usually) can be woven or knotted together. Pouring plaster is a good technique to teach—this is useful to crafts other than pottery. Chances are that the crafts you are working on in your curriculum have a relationship to clay.

We realize that many of these suggestions are idealistic. When you work in your own studio, you don't have to worry about when the bell rings, limited materials and equipment, bus schedules, budgets, and any number of daily hassles a school teacher encounters. If he gets the proper equipment and materials under control, he considers himself lucky. If, as an added bonus, the students are really motivated, he feels even more fortunate.

In a way, the hobbyist is in a similar situation. Usually he has limitations imposed by his equipment, or lack of it, and by his materials. In both cases, once the basic equipment and materials problems are sufficiently under control, some forward progress can be made, growth takes place, and satisfactory results occur. This will probably only happen after a certain amount of effort and frustration. It is our hope that the information and methods provided in this book will minimize the frustration involved in "getting into pots" and that the time spent will sooner lead to satisfaction and enjoyment.

APPENDIX A

Suppliers

There seem to be as many suppliers opening up as there are craft shops. We have included names of some that we or our friends have dealt with.

There are also *listings* of suppliers appearing regularly on the market—we have included some of the listings as well as some of the actual suppliers. Also check the yellow pages of your telephone directory. You can eliminate shipping costs if you do business close to home.

Although you are not involved in hobby ceramics, some of the equipment and materials you will be using are the same.

Do not overlook hobby ceramics suppliers as a source of pottery supplies, especially if you are a small-volume hobby potter.

If ordering for schools, some suppliers seem to be better equipped to handle the shipping and billing procedures and the larger volume required for the school situation as opposed to the part-time hobby potter. Generally, you will have better luck going through large *general* suppliers than ordering directly from various manufacturers yourself. See Section II for more complete consumer information and advice.

LISTINGS OF CERAMICS SUPPLIERS

Ceramic Scope (former *Potluck Publications*)
P.O. Box 48643 (or 6363 Wilshire Blvd.)
Los Angeles, California   90048

This is almost a yellow pages for pottery and hobby ceramics. For example, Group 5 (p. 62), "Kilns, Potters Wheels, Firing Supplies" includes suppliers of firebrick, automatic controls, elements, electric kilns, gas kilns, pyrometers, repair service, shelves, thermocouples, timers, and wheels (electric, kick, kit, etc.). The *Buyers Guide* is published yearly and costs $4—an excellent investment for the consumer of pottery equipment and supplies.

Ceramics Monthly
Box 4548
Columbus, Ohio   43212

Many suppliers and distributors advertise regularly in this magazine for potters. A subscription costs $8 a year.

LISTINGS OF GENERAL CRAFTS SUPPLIERS

Contemporary Crafts Market Place
44 W. 53 St.
New York, New York   10019

Compiled by the American Crafts Council, this is a 502-page soft-cover guide to craft suppliers, classes, audiovisual materials, reference publications, shops and galleries, organizations, calendars, and periodicals.

Craft Sources: The Ultimate Catalog for Craftspeople
by Paul Colin and Deborah Lippman
M. Evans & Co., Inc., New York. 240 pp.
Hard cover: $12.50; Soft cover: $5.95

Craft Supplies Supermarket
by Joseph Rosenbloom
Oliver Press, Willits, California
205 pp. Soft cover: $3.95

National Guide to Craft Supplies (The Craft Yellow Pages)
by Judith Glassman
Van Nostrand Reinhold Co., New York.
205 pp. Hard cover: $19.95; Soft cover: $6.95

GENERAL CERAMICS (POTTERY) SUPPLIERS

Here we have cited suppliers who we or people we know have dealt with. Look for suppliers close to you so you can reduce shipping costs. There are many more, but those listed carry a wide range of materials and equipment for the studio potter.

West Coast:
Western Ceramic Supply
1601 Howard St.
San Francisco, California   94103

Midwest:
Minnesota Clay Company
8001 Grand Ave. South
Bloomington, Minnesota   55420

Rovin Ceramics
6912 Schaefer Road
Dearborn, Michigan   48126

Amaco—American Art Clay Co.
4717 W. 16 St.
Indianapolis, Indiana   46222

East Coast:
Newton Pottery Supply Co.
96 Rumford Ave.
West Newton, Massachusetts   02158

Miller Ceramics
8934 N. Seneca St.
Weedsport, New York   13166

Standard Ceramic Supply Co.
Box 4435
Pittsburgh, Pennsylvania   15205

SUPPLIERS OF
SPECIFIC THINGS

Chemicals and Glaze Materials:
Ceramic Color and Chemical
    Manufacturing
P.O. Box 297
New Brighton, Pennsylvania   15066

Silicon Carbide Shelves:
New Castle Refractories
New Castle, Pennsylvania   16101
(Sells firsts and seconds and won't ship.)

Pug Mills and Mixers:
Bluebird Mfg. Co.
100 Gregory Rd.
Ft. Collins, Colorado   80521

Creek Turn Lab
Rte. 38
Hainesport, New Jersey   08036

Gas Analyzers:
Bacharach Instrument Co.
625 Alpha Drive
RIDC Industrial Park
Pittsburgh, Pennsylvania   15238
(Zero to 20% CO_2, # 10-5,000)

Glaze
Recipes

RAKU GLAZES
(919°C OR 1686°F)

The following two tables show good base glazes for Raku—neither one contains lead. The Raku base uses colemanite (gerstley borate) as the main flux; the fritted Raku base uses a frit.

Add 2% bentonite to keep glaze materials in suspension. See Chapter 14 for discussion of oxides with these base glazes.

RAKU BASE

Colemanite	75%
Spar (C-6)	20%
Borax	5%

FRITTED RAKU BASE

Colemanite	30%
Spar	20%
Frit P-311	50%

OXIDATION GLAZES

The following electric kiln glazes (04 and 7) were tested in a small electric kiln with an automatic shut-off. In a kiln without a shut-off, this is equivalent to cones 05 and 6 (one cone lower than for automatic). All glazes have enough tolerance that this isn't terribly critical but may affect the surface slightly.

Cone 04-05 Electric (1098°C or 2008°F). Note that these glazes contain no lead which is toxic. Barium carbonate in its prefired form is also toxic—so be careful, or avoid it.

Read *down* the lettered columns:

CONE 04–05 OXIDATION GLAZES

Glaze Materials	A	B	J	S	Y	Z
Frit P–311 (F3124, H90)	40	30	55	60		
Dolomite				15		
Kaolin or Ball Clay		10	10	15		
Flint	37	35	15	10	36	25
Whiting	12	15	5			12
Zinc Oxide	11	10	15			
Colemanite (gerstley borate)					32	22
Nepheline Syenite					32	
Spar (C–6)						38
Barium Carbonate					5	5
Bentonite (suspender)	2	2	2	2	2	2
	satin	satin	shiny	satin	shiny	satin

Oxide Additions: The previous glazes take normal coloring oxides well. For blue, use cobalt, which will turn turquoise in zinc base glazes. For green, use chrome or copper. For toast, use rutile. For brown, use manganese. For mustard, use iron.

Try 3–5% of most oxides as a starting point. For chrome and cobalt, try 1%.

For bright, primary colors at this temperature, try glaze stains.

Cone 6-7 Electric (1255°C or 2291°F). For a more detailed description, see Chapter 11 on electric kiln firing.

CONE 6-7 OXIDATION GLAZES

	C–6	X–S	SH	C6W	18
Feldspar	45	40	50	33	40
Whiting	18	20	10		15
Kaolin or Ball Clay	25	10	20	25	20
Zinc Oxide	12	5	10	12	
Silica (flint)		20			15
Zircopax (added to base)		20			
Talc			15		
Wollastonite				30	
Dolomite					10
	matt	shiny	shiny	satin–matt	satin

The first-column glaze, C–6, is a super all-purpose matt glaze for this temperature. C–6 alone is a good, light-colored, matt glaze. With 3% copper, it is green (with more, it approaches black). With 3% manganese dioxide, it turns a nice brown color. If C–6, which has had oxides added, is used in combination with C–6, X–S, or C6W bases, nice, broken-up, mottled surfaces occur.

REDUCTION GLAZES

Cone 10 (1305°C or 2381°F). See Chapter
13 on reduction firing for more details.

CONE 10 REDUCTION GLAZES

	R–32	Wt–b	Sp.M.	Liner	Ash
Feldspar					
Oxford (potash)	48.9				
C–6 (soda)		45	30	41	40
Dolomite	22.4	25	25	7	
Clay					
kaolin	25.1				
ball clay		25	25	5	20
Nepheline Syenite		10			
Whiting	3.5	5			
Spodumene			20		
Zircopax			15		
Flint				20	
Talc				15	
Colemanite				12	
Fireplace Ashes					40
	very dry	waxy	waxy	satin–	fluid–
	opaque	matt	matt	shiny	matt–shiny
	matt		rust–tan		
			cream		

APPENDIX C

Glossary of Materials

CLAY MATERIALS

Our cone 10 stoneware body contains 40% fireclay (A.P. Green 20 mesh), 35% stoneware clay (Cedar Heights Gold Art), 12% ball clay (C and C); 5% silica (flint), 8% feldspar (C–6, a soda spar), and 2–5% grog.

The following partial list explains the difference between kinds of clays. All clays have the theoretical formula:

$$Al_2O_3 \cdot 2SiO_2 \cdot 2H_2O$$

Ball Clay is a light burning clay of high plasticity because of its fine particle size. It is added to stoneware or fire clays to make them more throwable. An addition of 10–15% is normal. Too much ball clay will increase shrinkage and often lead to cracking problems.

Stoneware and Fire Clays are clays with coarser particles. They mature at high temperatures.

Earthenware Clays tend to be red due to the iron oxide in them and fire to maturity at lower temperatures: cone 08–02. They are relatively fragile and porous when fired as opposed to stoneware clays which approach a vitreous (non-porous) state when fired. Most of the clays found in nature are earthenware—and most pottery the world over has been made of earthenware clay. It is also the material for bricks. (Our cone 10 body has no earthenware clay in it.)

Kaolin or China Clay is a white clay; somewhat similar to a ball clay but having larger particles and not as plastic. It is used in porcelain, because it fires white. (It is also taken internally and is the "kao" part of kaopectate.) There is no china clay in our stoneware clay body.

Grog is a nonplastic material used in a clay body to give it a more open structure and to give it more "tooth" for pulling on the wheel. It tends to feel gritty. Grog is clay which has been fired once and ground back up again. It is usually made from fireclay and comes in varying particle sizes. We use 30–40 mesh grog in our clay body.

Flint and Feldspar are ingredients in a stoneware body, but they are not clays. See Glaze materials for further explanation.

GLAZE MATERIALS

Here are the materials we have mentioned in giving you glaze recipes (cone 04, cone 6, and cone 10 reduction). A glaze is basically composed of *flint, clay, feldspar,* and other fluxes.

1. *Flint* (silica, SiO_2) is the most important ingredient in glaze. It is the glass former. It also improves the fit of glaze to pot and reduces the problem of crazing.

2. *Clay* is discussed previously as to formula and types. Ball clay or kaolin is used in glazes as a source of alumina— the hardener. It makes the glaze more viscous and prevents its running off the pot. The clay in a glaze also acts as a suspending agent—keeping the particles from settling out and sinking to the bottom of the bucket.

3. *Feldspar* is very important in stoneware glazes. It is similar to clay in that it is composed of alumina and silica (in different proportions, though, than found in clay). Unlike clay, it contains at least one flux— soda and potash predominantly. Feldspar contains

one flux	+	one alumina	+	6 silica
Na_2O or K_2O		Al_2O_3		$6SiO_2$

If it contains more soda, it is generally referred to as a *soda spar.* If the flux is predominantly potash, it is commonly called a *potash spar.* Soda is a stronger flux than potash.

Feldspar will melt, by itself, to a stiff glaze at cone 10, and many good stoneware glazes are nearly all feldspar.

Nepheline Syenite: As you can see by the formula,

$$\begin{matrix} .75\ Na_2O \\ .25\ K_2O \end{matrix} \quad Al_2O_3 \cdot 4SiO_2$$

nepheline syelite is a feldspathic material. It is high in soda and has less silica than feldspar, so it fuses at a lower temperature and acts as a very good flux. In general: If you replace the feldspar in a cone 9–10 glaze with nepheline syenite, you come very close to getting a cone 6 glaze.

Spodumene is a lithium feldspar, similar to nepheline syenite, with lithia replacing soda in the formula as the flux.

4. *Fluxes:*

Whiting ($CaCO_3$) is the most desirable fluxing ingredient in stoneware glazes (up to 15%). It has a low thermal expansion and fluxes a glaze without causing it to craze.

Dolomite ($CaCO_3 \cdot MgCO_3$) contains equal amounts of calcia and magnesia, nature's blend, which is better than if combined artificially. It is a flux, like whiting ($CaCO_3$), and usually used along with, not in place of, whiting. We use 25% dolomite in our cone 10 matt base glaze. It tends to turn cobalt purple or lavender instead of blue, so be cautioned to avoid "magnesia base" glazes with blues.

Zinc Oxide (ZnO) is a powerful flux when used in fairly small quantities. It has a low coefficient of expansion which helps counteract crazing. Zinc may induce crawling—use calcined zinc oxide to avoid this problem.

Barium Carbonate ($BaCO_3$) is a fluxing material and matting agent used in glazes; it also influences coloring oxides. Barium matt glazes at cone 10 can be very effective. It is toxic in its raw, prefered state.

Talc ($3MgO/4SiO_2/H_2O$) is like a flux. It is used when both magnesia and silica are required in a glaze, since it is a natural blend of the two.

Colemanite ($2CaO/3B_2O_3/5H_2O$) is a calcium boron compound which is a strong flux. Gerstley borate is the commercial replacement for colemanite. Colemanite plus rutile at cone 10 reduction will give a mottled bluish effect.

Frits are glazes which have been fired once, cooled, and ground into powder. They melt at a low temperature, are useful in Raku and cone 04 glazes to avoid lead compounds, and are very stable. Glassy.

Coloring Oxides. Some of the more common oxides which can be added to a base glaze to give it color are: iron, chrome, copper, cobalt, rutile, manganese, illmenite (Chs. 11, 12, App. B). In reduction firing, the oxides are "reduced" by the oxygen-starved atmosphere of the kiln. Some oxides, especially copper, give entirely different colors (red vs. green) in reduction versus oxidation firing. For a comprehensive analysis of different oxides and what they do, see *Clay and Glazes for the Potter,* by Daniel Rhodes. Normally blue can be obtained with cobalt oxide; browns and rusts with iron oxide; greens with copper and chrome oxides; whites with tin, zircopax, or other opacifiers; yellow with vanadium stain, etc. Two or more coloring oxides can be used in combination for some effects. The final color will depend on the base glaze and the temperature and atmosphere in the kiln, as well as on the clay body of the pot—in addition to the coloring oxide(s) used.

Glossary of Terms

absorption (absorbency) The taking up of liquid into the pores of a pot. The water absorption of a ceramic material is an indication of its degree of vitrification.

aging of clay Letting clay sit for a period of time after mixing for attainment of full plasticity.

alkali Refers mainly to soda, potash, and lithia. Alkalis are strong fluxes and combine with silica at relatively low temperatures.

ash glaze A glaze that contains large proportions (up to 50%) of wood ash, which acts as a flux. Normally fired to stoneware temperatures.

atmosphere The ambient air inside a kiln during firing. There are three basic atmospheres: oxidation, neutral, and reduction. An oxidizing atmosphere occurs in any kiln fired with an ample supply of oxygen. In an electric kiln, the atmosphere is usually oxidizing. Neutral is the theoretical dividing point between oxidation and reduction. A neutral atmosphere results from perfect combustion in a fuel burning kiln. A reducing atmosphere contains insufficient oxygen for complete combustion. Reduction is usually accomplished in a fuel burning kiln.

bag wall (*see* fire box)

banding The application of a band of color to a pot. A brush dipped in wax or stain is held perfectly still on the pot's surface as it turns on the wheel.

banding wheel Normally a portable turntable on which the pot to be banded is centered and spun. A potters wheel can also be used for this. Banding wheels are useful for rotating handbuilt pots during construction or decoration.

bat Thick (usually plaster) plate, which fits into the wheel head, upon which centering, etc., can be directly performed.

batch Ingredients of a glaze formula measured in proper proportions for blending.

bisque (biscuit) Unglazed ware which has had a preliminary firing.

bone dry Dried completely and ready for bisque-firing (fragile).

burnishing The polishing of the surface of a leather-hard pot with a smooth tool.

calcine To heat a ceramic material to the temperature necessary to drive out the chemical water and other volatile materials.

calipers A tool with adjustable curved arms for measuring the diameter of a pot. Most frequently used for the fitting of lids.

centering Applying pressure to a ball of clay

on the wheel as it revolves, to persuade the whole mass to run true.

ceramic From the Greek term ''keramos''— ware made from clay and fired. Current technical and scientific usage has broadened the definition considerably, and it now has so wide an application as to have lost much of its meaning.

chatter Corrugation of the surface of clay which can develop during trimming. It can be caused by clay which is too hard (or occasionally too soft), a slack hold on the tool, etc. Chatter can be avoided or corrected by use of a *Surform* tool.

chemical water Water chemically combined in the clay molecule as opposed to the physical water which is added to dry clay. It is driven off at 500–600°C, altering the molecular pattern and forming a new material.

chuck As applied to trimming, a support for pots which would otherwise be unstable, such as bottles with narrow necks.

closed form A form similar to a bottle but further constricted so no opening is left.

coiling An age-old technique of building pots by laying coils or ropes of clay one on top of the other and working them together.

collaring Constricting the neck of a bottle *after* it has been thrown and your hand has been removed from the inside. Performed by encircling bottle with thumb and index and second fingers of both hands, pressing inward, and slowly sliding upward.

combing Decoration by scoring with a toothed or pronged instrument. In its wider sense, the term also applies to sgraffito-like decoration through slip or glaze.

cone A small toothlike pyramid made of clay and glaze materials, which melts at a specific temperature due to size of cone and rate at which kiln is heated. Referred to with numbers that indicate melting temperatures. For example, firing to cone 6 means heating the kiln until it reaches 1250°C and then shutting it off.

cone plaque or handmade ''pat.'' A base into which three successive cones have been stuck (the middle one indicating the desired firing temperature). These are placed in front of the peephole to determine when to shut the kiln off and can also be positioned in various parts of the kiln to check for uniformity of temperature.

coning Constricting the diameter of the walls *before* they have been pulled up, just after opening and widening the clay mass. Performed by edge of thumb sliding up the wall and pushing it in toward the center. (See Figs. 2–15 and 2–16.)

crawling A glaze fault—the separation of the glaze coating during firing causing some unglazed areas to be exposed.

crazing A network of fractures in a glaze caused by differences in contraction between body and glaze during cooling.

crystalline (See matt glaze)

cut-off string Wire, fish line, or dental floss usually attached at both ends to small dowels. Held taut, it is passed under a thrown pot in order to release and remove the pot from the bat or wheel head.

damp box An airtight cupboard where pots can be stored to prevent further drying or to equalize their moisture content.

deflocculation The dispersion of particles especially in a clay slip leading to increased fluidity. This is achieved by the use of an electrolyte, usually sodium in silicate or carbonate form.

dunting The formation of cracks, which may be invisible, in a pot cooled too rapidly or unevenly after it has been fired.

engobe White or colored clay slip used to decorate pots at the leather-hard state.

epsom salts Magnesium sufate can be added in small quantities to glazes as a suspending agent. (*see also* flocculate)

eutectic Mixtures that have a fusion temperature lower than that of any of the individual components.

fat clay Clay that is plastic (very throwable).

fire box The combustion chamber in a fuel-burning kiln.

firebrick An insulation brick that withstands high temperatures. Usually made from fire clay.

firing The process of heating pots in a kiln to a specific temperature. (*see* atmosphere, reduction firing, *and* oxidation firing).

flange A narrow ledge at the rim of the pot for seating a lid.

flocculate To thicken a slip or glaze so that it needs more water to render it fluid. Epsom salts is a flocculant.

flux A substance which causes or promotes melting.

foot A low pedestal which can be trimmed into the base of a leather-hard pot, especially a bowl.

frit (*see* Appendix C under Glaze Materials).

fyrite (CO₂) *analyzer* A sampling device which measures the CO_2 in the kiln's atmosphere to determine the amount of reduction taking place.

glaze A thin glassy surface coating applied to a pot to decorate it or seal the pores. The term *glaze* can also refer to the liquid suspension of finely ground materials that is ready to be applied to the surface.

glaze-body fit Refers to the difference in expansion between the glaze and body. A glaze that fits does not craze or shiver.

greenware Bone-dry pots ready for bisque-firing.

grog (*see* Clay Materials in Appendix C)

kiln A furnace made of refractory clay materials for firing ceramic products.

kiln cement A mixture of fireclay and sodium silicate for mending kiln linings.

kiln elements Kanthal wire heating coils installed in grooved firebrick walls of electric kilns.

kiln furniture Refractory pieces used to support pots during firing. Shelves, posts and stilts are the most common.

kiln guard A back-up safety device for shutting off current to an electric kiln.

kiln setter An automatic device to shut off a kiln that is activated by the melting of a cone.

kilnwash A protective coating of refractory materials applied to the top surface of the kiln shelves to prevent glaze from sticking the ware to the shelf. An inexpensive kilnwash can be made by mixing equal parts of kaolin and flint with water.

lead glaze A low-temperature glaze containing lead as its main flux, with potential toxic hazards.

leather hard Clay that is dry enough to hold shape yet "moist" enough to be trimmed, carved, or scored.

lug Small handle on the side of a pot. Can be used to attach bamboo handles to teapots.

majolica The painting with oxides on a white earthenware glaze.

matt glaze A glaze with a smooth but non-shiny surface. Matt glazes are usually due to the development of very small surface crystals. Slow cooling in the upper temperature range is important.

mishima A form of inlay originating in Korea. The design is impressed into the clay at leather hard and then filled with brushed-on slip, which may or may not be scraped flat.

mold A form over which, or into which, a slab of clay can be placed to conform to the shape of the object. Includes hump molds, drape molds, press molds, etc. Molds can also be used for slip casting.

needle A fine awl for cutting clay, especially rims of thrown pots.

neutral fire (*see* atmosphere)

opacifier Oxides such as tin which are added to transparent glazes to make them opaque. Zircopax is also a commercially available opacifier.

opaque glaze When light cannot pass through a glaze but is reflected back from its surface, the glaze is termed *opaque*. Opacity is caused either by reflective matter suspended in the glaze, or by an uneven (matt) surface.

oxidation firing Firing pots in a kiln with an ample amount of oxygen; generally results in clearer, more specific, sometimes shinier glaze colors than those produced by reduction firing. (*see* atmosphere).

oxide The colorant in clay bodies and glazes; usually metallic, such as cobalt, iron, or chrome oxide. (See *also* Coloring Oxides in Appendix C.)

peephole An opening left in a kiln wall for observing the firing and viewing the cones.

pinholing A defect found most often in stoneware glazes which remain quite viscous at high temperatures.

plaster of Paris Powdered calcined gypsum, which, when recombined with water, sets up into an absorbent solid. Used in pottery for throwing-bats as well as for molds.

plastic Very throwable clay comprised by weight of ¼ water and ¾ clay; dependent on amount of fine-particled clay in body.

plasticity The quality of moist clay, which determines the amount of manipulation possible without cracking and the clay's ability to maintain a new shape when pressure is removed.

porcelain A translucent white clay body, usually containing approximately 50% kaolin, 25% flint and 25% feldspar, which is fired to vitrification.

porosity (*see* absorption)

pottery, pots Fired clay objects, usually made by hand. The root *pot* applies generally to containers. Pottery can also refer to the place where the pots are made.

pug mill A machine for consolidating plastic clay and extruding it into a firm column.

pyrometer An instrument for measuring heat at high temperatures.

pyrometric cone (*see* cone)

raw glaze A glaze composed of nonfritted materials.

reducing agent In the kiln's atmosphere, carbon monoxide and hydrogen. As a glaze component, silicon carbide.

reduction firing Firing pots in an oxygen-starved atmosphere, accomplished by increasing the amount of fuel and decreasing the amount of air flowing into the kiln. The chemical reaction between the extra carbon monoxide and hydrogen molecules from the excess fuel and the oxides in the glazes generally results in earth tones and muted colors in fired pots. (*see* atmosphere)

refractory Heat-resistant ceramic material. Kiln refractories include bricks, shelves, and furniture.

rib A tool used to aid in shaping the pot.

salt glaze A glaze achieved by throwing salt into the kiln at high temperatures.

score To scratch a leather-hard pot before adding slip (wet clay) in order to securely attach other pieces of clay. Also called *crosshatching*.

screen (*sieve*) A wire mesh dish for sieving materials; available in calibrated sizes.

sgraffito Decoration by incising or scratching through slip or glaze to reveal the background color or material.

short clay Clay that is not plastic enough for easy throwing.

shrinkage Contraction of clay during drying and firing.

silica (SiO_2) also called flint. (*see* Glaze Materials in Appendix C)

silicon carbide The excellent refractoriness of this material makes it useful for kiln shelves used at high temperatures.

silicosis A lung disease caused by clay dust inhaled over a long period of time.

slab A rolled flat section of clay used for handbuilding.

slip Clay in liquid suspension. Deflocculated slip is used in casting. Slip is also used after scoring in joining clay sections. Colored slip can be used decoratively and is usually called an *engobe*.

slip clay A naturally occurring clay with sufficient fluxing ingredients to melt to a glaze at stoneware temperatures. Albany slip is the most notable example.

slip trailer A device for extruding a thin trail of slip or engobe for surface decoration.

slumping The collapse of a pot in a kiln due to overfiring.

sprigging Decorating the surface of a leather-hard pot by applying a bas-relief made in a small press mold.

stacked A loaded kiln that is ready for heating.

stain Any oxide or prepared pigment used for coloring bodies, slips, or glazes. Also, oxides dissolved in water and applied with a brush for signing or decorating pots.

stamp To impress a texture into soft clay with

a hard stamp; or, to print a colored pattern on clay or glaze by means of a rubber stamp.

stilt (*see* kiln furniture)

stoneware High-fired ware with slight or no absorbency. Similar to porcelain but containing color impurities. (*Stoneware clay: see* Clay Materials in Appendix C.)

string a pot To pass the cut-off string under a thrown pot. Also, to put rope through the holes of a fired pot for hanging.

Surform A wide flat blade that is useful for smoothing and shaping clay during trimming. Used normally in woodworking, similar to a plane.

suspending agent Epsom salts, bentonite, and ball clay will all act to keep glaze materials in suspension.

throwing The process of centering, opening, widening, coning, and pulling a moist lump of clay into a finished form.

trimming Smoothing or shaping the base of a pot in the leather-hard state on the wheel.

viscosity The nonrunning quality of a glaze at peak temperatures.

vitreous (Vitrify, vitrification) Glassy or con-taining glassy materials. A vitreous or vitrified body will have low porosity.

ware (*see* pottery)

warping Deformation which can take place at any stage in the making, drying, and firing of a pot.

wax resist A method of decorating pottery by brushing on a design with a wax solution. This will prevent an applied stain or glaze from adhering to the decorated areas. Wax can be brushed on a leather-hard pot to resist an engobe, on a bisqued pot to resist glaze, or on a glazed pot to resist a contrasting coating of glaze or stain.

wedging Kneading plastic clay in a rocking spiral motion to remove air pockets and develop a uniform texture.

wheel Potters wheels are of two basic designs —the traditional kick wheel with a heavy fly wheel, and the more recent power wheel driven by a self-contained electric motor.

wheel head A metal disc which can be thrown on directly or can be adapted for removable bats.

Bibliography

There are hundreds of pottery books on the market, and more of them keep appearing regularly. We have listed a good basic reference library, which costs about $100, plus many other available books on pottery and related subjects. For an even more comprehensive list, write to the American Crafts Council, 44 W. 53rd St., New York, N.Y. 10019. They publish a lengthy bibliography in "clay" and will send it to you for a small fee.

A GOOD BASIC REFERENCE LIBRARY FOR $100

Ball, F. Carlton, *Syllabus for Beginning Pottery,* Bassett, Calif.: Keramos Books, 1971. ($3.95)

_____, *Syllabus for Advanced Ceramics,* Bassett, Calif.: Keramos Books, 1972. ($3.95)

_____, *Decorating Pottery with Clay Slip and Glaze,* Columbus, Ohio: Ceramics Monthly —Professional Publications, 1967 ($3.00)

These three books are well worth the $11 total cost. Carlton Ball is an excellent teacher, and his material is presented clearly and succinctly—very good sources for beginners.

_____, and Janice Lovoos, *Making Pottery without a Wheel, Texture and Form in Clay,* New York: Van Nostrand Reinhold, 1965.

Berensohn, Paulus, *Finding One's Way with Clay,* New York: Simon & Schuster, 1972. Excellent on coloring clays with oxides; pinching forms.

Colbeck, John, *Pottery, The Technique of Throwing,* New York: Watson-Guptill, and London, BT Batsford Ltd., 1969.

Fournier, Robert, *Illustrated Dictionary of Practical Pottery,* New York: Van Nostrand Reinhold, 1973. A great reference book; pottery terms and techniques explained clearly and listed alphabetically; many photos.

Nelson, Glenn C., *Ceramics, A Potter's Handbook,* New York: Holt, Rinehart & Winston, 1971. A classic; thorough, well-illustrated; perhaps a bit difficult for the beginner in sections but worth growing into.

Olsen, Frederick L., *The Kiln Book,* Bassett, Calif.: Keramos Books, 1973. Don't build your own kiln without reading this book first.

Rhodes, Daniel, *Clay and Glazes for the Potter,* Phila., Pa.: Chilton, 1968. Dan Rhodes is so articulate the books don't even need photos (which they don't have); superlative on clay and glaze materials—a stretch for the beginner. Another classic. His other two books are good too.

Rothenberg, Polly, *The Complete Book of Ceramic Art,* New York: Crown, 1972. Inspirational photos; sections on plaster and raku are especially good.

Wettlaufer, George and Nancy, *The Craftsman's Survival Manual,* Englewood Cliffs, N.J.: Prentice-Hall, Inc., 1974. In all modesty, if you're going to be selling your work, this book is certainly worth $2.95.

Winterburn, Mollie, *The Technique of Hand-built Pottery,* New York: Watson-Guptill, 1966. Beautiful, great for working with kids too.

Note: The books not priced are mostly hardbounds and average out at about $10.00. We may have gone a little over the $100 budget.

GENERAL POTTERY BOOKS

Bagg, Graham, *Pottery Techniques On and Off the Wheel,* New York: Van Nostrand Reinhold, 1974.

Counts, Charles, *Pottery Workshop,* New York: The Macmillan Co., 1973.

*Fournier, Robert, *Illustrated Dictionary.*
_____, *Ceramic Creations,* Bonanza, 1971.

Hofsted, Jolyon, *Step by Step Ceramics,* Racine, Wisconsin: Golden Press, Western Publishing Co., 1967.

Kenny, John, *The Complete Book of Pottery Making,* Phila., Pa.: Chilton, 1949.

Leach, Bernard, *A Potter's Book,* Great Britain: Transatlantic Arts, 15th American printing, 1972.

*Nelson, Glenn C., *Ceramics, A Potter's Handbook.*

Pucci, Cora, *Pottery A Basic Manual,* Boston, Mass.: Little Brown, 1974.

*Rhodes, Daniel, *Clay and Glazes for the Potter.*

_____, *Stoneware and Porcelain,* Phila., Pa.: Chilton, 1959.

Richards, Mary C., *Centering in Pottery Poetry and Person,* Middletown, Conn.: Wesleyan University Press, 1962. Philosophy; not a how-to.

*Rothenberg, Polly, *The Complete Book of Ceramic Art.*

*Described in basic $100 library.

Sunset, *Ceramics, Techniques and Projects,* Menlo Park, Calif.: Lane, 1973.

Thorpe, Harold, *Basic Pottery for the Student,* New York: St. Martins Press, 1973. Contains a good chapter on design.

Zorza, Rosemary, *Pottery, Creating with Clay,* Garden City, N.Y.: Doubleday, 1974.

BOOKS FOR THOSE WORKING WITH CHILDREN IN CLAY
(Good for adults too)

Ceramics Monthly, *Ceramic Projects,* Columbus, Ohio: Professional Publications, 1963.

Farnworth, Warren, *Beginning Pottery,* New York: Van Nostrand Reinhold, 1973.

*Winterburn, Mollie, *The Technique of Handbuilt Pottery.*

BOOKS ON THROWING

*Colbeck, John, *Pottery the Technique of Throwing.*

Sellers, Thomas, *Throwing on the Potter's Wheel,* Columbus, Ohio: Professional Publications, 1960.

BOOKS ON HANDFORMING METHODS

*Ball, Carlton, and Janice Lovoos, *Making Pottery without a Wheel.*

*Berensohn, Paulus, *Finding One's Way with Clay.*

Priolo, Joan and Anthony, *Ceramics by Slab,* New York: Sterling, 1973.

BOOKS ON GLAZES

Behrens, Richard, *Glaze Projects,* ("A Formulary of Leadless Glazes"), Columbus, Ohio Professional Publications, 1971.

Fraser, Harry, *Glazes for the Craft Potter,* New York: Watson-Guptill, 1973.

Green, David, *Pottery Glazes,* New York, N.Y.: Watson-Guptill, 1973.

Luisi, Billie, *Potworks, A First Book of Clay,* New York: Morrow Paperback Editions, 1973. Not really a how-to, but a good book with a very clear section on developing glazes. Good for a beginner.

Sanders, Herbert, *Glazes for Special Effects,* New York: Watson-Guptill, 1974.

Singer, Felix, *Ceramic Glazes,* London: Borax Consolidated, 1960.

BOOKS ON KILNS

*Olsen, Frederick L., *The Kiln Book.*

Rhodes, Daniel, *Kilns, Design, Construction and Operation,* Phila., Pa.: Chilton, 1968.

BOOKS ON RAKU

Lynggaard, Finn, *Pottery: Raku Technique,* New York: Van Nostrand Reinhold, 1970.

Piepenburg, Robert, *Raku Pottery,* New York: The Macmillan Co., 1972.

Riegger, Hal, *Raku—Art and Technique,* New York: Van Nostrand Reinhold, 1970.

BOOKS ON INSTRUCTION

American Crafts Council, *Contemporary Crafts Market Place.* A guide to suppliers, classes, audio visual materials, etc. (*See* Appendix A.)

_____, "Directory of Craft Courses." A list available from the American Crafts Council for $2.50, 44 W. 53rd Street, New York, N.Y. 10019.

Coyne, John, and Tom Hebert, *By Hand—A Guide to Schools and a Career in Crafts,* New York: E.P. Dutton, 1974. A really good book for school guidance offices to have in their library and for individuals; arranged by state; gives courses available in schools as well as private studios.

BOOKS ON PHOTOGRAPHING CRAFTS

Barsness, John C., *Photographing Crafts,* $4.95, American Crafts Council, 44 W. 53rd St., New York, N.Y. 10019.

Schmid, Claus–Peter, *Photography for Artists and Craftsmen,* New York: Van Nostrand Reinhold, 1975. Super.

PERIODICALS ON CRAFTS AND CRAFTS MARKETING

The Goodfellow Newsletter and Catalog, Christopher Weills, ed., Box 4520, Berkeley, Calif. 94704.

The Working Craftsman, Marilyn Heise, ed., $9.00 a year, Box 42, Northbrook, Ill. 60062. Good marketing column by Michael Higgins.

The Crafts Report, "The Newsmonthly of Marketing, Management and Money for Crafts Professionals," Michael Scott, ed., $11 a year, 116 University Pl., New York, N.Y. 10003.

Craft Horizons, publication of The American Crafts Council, 44 W. 53 St., New York, N.Y. 10019.

MAGAZINES ON POTTERY

Ceramics Monthly, $8.00 a year, Box 12448, Columbus, Ohio 43212.

Studio Potter, Gerry Williams, ed., subscription $6.00 a year, published semi-annually, Box 172, Warner, N.H. 03278.

TECHNICAL BOOKS

Kingery, W.D., *Ceramic Fabrication Processes,* Cambridge, Mass.: M.I.T. Press, 1963.

Kirkendale, George, *Firing Ceramics,* SUNY, Alfred, Feb. 1968.

_____, Drying Claywares, Feb. 1967.

Lawrence, G.W., *Ceramic Science for the Potter,* Phila., Pa.: Chilton, 1972.

North American Manufacturing Co., *Combustion Handbook,* Cleveland, Ohio, 1952.

Norton, F.H. *Elements of Ceramics,* Cambridge, Mass.: Addison-Wesley, 1952.

_____, *Ceramics for the Artist Potter,* Cambridge, Mass.: Addison-Wesley, 1956.

_____, *Fine Ceramics,* New York: McGraw-Hill Book Co., 1970.

Parmelee, Cullen W., *Ceramic Glazes,* Chicago, Ill.: Industrial Pub., 1951.

Index

*Boldface page numbers indicate photographs or artwork.